DISPLAY

A Handbook of Elementary Classroom Ideas to Motivate the Creation of Bulletin Boards

AUTHOR

LUCY L. LAURAIN

PUBLISHED BY
EDUCATIONAL SERVICE, INC.
P.O. BOX 219
Stevensville, Michigan 49127

TABLE OF CONTENTS

PAGE

SECTION I: "BULLETIN BOARD READINESS"
General Information 3
Special Boards 6
Materials 7

SECTION II: "LANGUAGE ARTS"
1. Vowels 13
2. Feel The Word 13
3. Sight Words 14
4. Odd Man Out 15
5. Make Your Word Garden Grow 16
6. Where Shall I Look? 17
7. Critical Thinking 19
8. SQ3R = Better Learning 20
9. Newspaper Services 21
10. Want Ads 22
11. Potpourri 23
12. Jiminy Cricket! 24
13. Good Spelling 25
14. Foolish And Funny 25
15. Comic Caper 26
16. Superstitions 27
17. How Wise R U? 28
18. Brew Up An Interest In Reading 29
19. A Good Listener 31
20. How Do We Listen? 31
21. Spelling Scramble 33
22. Monster Of The Day! 33
23. Don't Be Spooked! 34
24. Prefixes 35
25. Compound Words 36
26. Antonyms Are An Open And Shut Case 37
27. Homonyms 38
28. Dictionary Daisies 39
29. Mail Call 41
30. Punctuation 42

31. Good Grammar.............................. 44
32. Make A Sentence........................... 45
33. Paragraph Wagon 46
34. Parts Of Speech Names 46
35. Parts Of Speech Uses 47
36. Haiku 49
37. Books We Read.............................. 50
38. The Web Of Mystery 51
39. Sign In Please!.............................. 52
40. The Library Windmill Of My Mind 53
41. The Card Catalog 54

SECTION III: "SOCIAL STUDIES"

1. Community Helpers 57
2. Tools We Use 58
3. What Shall I Be?........................... 58
4. Transportation.............................. 59
5. Our Place On The Earth.................... 60
6. Hang In There 61
7. Latitude And Longitude 62
8. The United States 64
9. Indians Of North America 65
10. Secrets Of Plymouth Rock.................. 66
11. Early Colonial Life......................... 67
12. Portraits Of Liberty 68
13. Presidents 69
14. Revoltin' Reasons 69
15. The Civil War.............................. 70
16. World Wars................................. 71
17. Wartime 72
18. Who Stepped Where 73
19. Our Government............................ 74
20. Capital Cities.............................. 75
21. Around The World 77
22. Royalty..................................... 77
23. People And Places......................... 78
24. Collage 79
25. Light Up A Fact 79

SECTION IV: "MATH"

		PAGE
1.	Add The Dominoes	83
2.	Counting	83
3.	Number Folks	85
4.	Place Value	86
5.	Mayan Numbers	87
6.	Roman Numerals	88
7.	Big And Little	89
8.	What Do You Mean?	90
9.	Sets	90
10.	Grocery Shopping	91
11.	Time Tables	93
12.	Division Talk	96
13.	Fractions	97
14.	The Puzzle Of Fractions	98
15.	Equivalents	99
16.	Ratio	100
17.	Money	101
18.	Banking	102
19.	Calendar Time	103
20.	Telling Time	104
21.	Measurement	105
22.	The Metric System	106
23.	Geometric Figures	107
24.	P = Perimeter	108
25.	A = Area	109
26.	Area Of A Circle	110
27.	Bone Up On _____	111
28.	Snow Job	113

SECTION V: "SCIENCE"

1.	The Animal Kingdom	117
2.	Be Informed About Biological Sciences	117
3.	Undersea World	118
4.	Classification Of Plants	119
5.	Tree Talk	121
6.	Flower Parts	122
7.	Open The Doors To Good Nutrition	123

		PAGE
8.	Good Health	125
9.	Good Grooming	126
10.	Brush Your Teeth Often	127
11.	Cross Section Of A Tooth	128
12.	Blood	129
13.	Add-A-Bone	130
14.	Fluoroscope	131
15.	Puzzle Of The Mind	132
16.	The Physical Sciences	132
17.	Chemical Elements	133
18.	Heat	134
19.	Thermometers	135
20.	Magnets	136
21.	Rocks	137
22.	Treasures Of The Earth	138
23.	Weather Map	138
24.	Precipitation	139
25.	Speed Of Light	140
26.	Beyond The Earth	141
27.	The Universe	142
28.	Look Up	143
29.	A Prism	144
30.	Ecology	145
31.	Ecology Is Now	146
32.	Bright Ideas	147

SECTION VI: "JUST BECAUSE"

1.	Fall	151
2.	Wintertime Is Funtime	151
3.	Spring Is Here!	152
4.	Shades Of Summer	153
5.	Safety Signs For "Cyclists"	154
6.	Far Away	156
7.	Play It Cool	157
8.	Lincoln-Washington	158
9.	Halloween	159
10.	Thanksgiving	159

		PAGE
11.	Joy To The World	160
12.	Happy Easter	161
13.	Religious Celebrations	162
14.	Color Board	163
15.	Months	164
16.	Telephones	166
17.	Telephone Directories	169
18.	Put-Ons	171

SECTION VII: "LETTERING"

Lettering 175

ACKNOWLEDGMENTS

A special thank you to the Redford Union School District for providing the time for me to work on this book. Also, I am grateful for the use of their curriculum guides used as resource materials.

Many thanks to the teachers I contacted to check on terminology, grade level, etc. I am especially grateful to Mrs. Rosemary Gould who supplied so much math information.

However, my highest praise and deepest appreciation is reserved for my husband, Ted, who was so patient, understanding and helpful while I worked on this project.

INTRODUCTION

DISPLAY joins the SPICE Series of handbooks published by Educational Service, Inc. The SPICE Series provides teachers with practical ideas and activities that enrich their teaching programs.

DISPLAY was developed for the elementary teacher to stimulate the creation of bulletin board displays that will motivate the children in their learning process. After basic information is presented on bulletin board preparation, type of boards to be used and materials to be used, ideas are given to encompass specific academic areas-language arts, social studies, mathematics, science and boards that are created "Just Because." Each display includes a description of all necessary materials, directions for assembly and suggestions for use. The material was condensed as much as possible in order to include many different display ideas within the space limitations of a truly functional handbook.

It is hoped that you will view the ideas you find in DISPLAY as a basis for bulletin board displays that will motivate the learning of your students.

SECTION I: "BULLETIN BOARD READINESS"

Section I will give you many ideas on what materials to use and how to set up boards in special classrooms. It should help you be prepared for bulletin board displays in any specific subject areas.

GENERAL INFORMATION

Simplicity, novelty and timing are three keys to effective bulletin boards.

Few teachers have the time, nor should they spend an excessive amount of time, preparing bulletin board materials. The displays should be durable, but easy to assemble. Make them of materials that can be saved for future use. Anything that can't be saved should be easy to duplicate.

Whenever possible, have the students put up the displays. Use their ideas, but make sure their goals are realistic. If necessary, help the students revise their fanciful ideas into workable ideas. (Without guidance, some students could take all year to put up a board. Beware of this pitfall!)

A bulletin board should act as a magnet and draw the student to it. There are many ways to achieve this. Not only are bulletin boards decorative, but they should stimulate learning.

Make boards reflect the community itself so students can relate to them. Be cognizant of special terminology. Just as one would not use "baby" words in a school for the gifted, one should not use college graduate words in other situations. Keep up with the latest slang. As any teacher knows, slang should not be encouraged as a permanent speech pattern, but it can be used for "shock value" on a bulletin board. Rarely, but for special effect, "big" words or obviously wrong wordage may be used.

Use current topics and ideas. Make the displays a sign of the times. Jump on the band wagon and be prepared, not just for holidays, but for a "happening." Use different ideas and materials. Don't be afraid to experiment!

Avoid the usual color schemes and try something a little more daring. In fact, try an "ugly" board sometime. A board can be made so atrocious that the students are drawn to it. They won't believe what they are seeing! (Caution — don't leave this board up for a long period of time.)

Contrary to the preceding statements, the bulletin board should be pleasing to the eye. Unity and design are important. Through the use of certain techniques, ideas can be tied together.

1. Have objects touch one another.

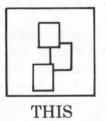
THIS

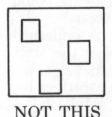
NOT THIS

2. Use twine, yarn or felt pen to tie the display together.

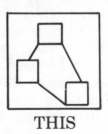
THIS

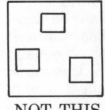
NOT THIS

3. Use paper and color to unite the display.

 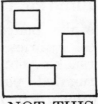

THIS   NOT THIS

4. Odd-numbered objects (flowers, flower petals, pictures, etc.,) are more interesting than an even-numbered display.

THIS   NOT THIS

Since most students are curious, make the board durable and touchable. A fragile display will start to fall apart (and the students will tend to help it along) and lose its effectiveness. Change the displays frequently before the materials become stale. Sometimes, looking at the same thing for weeks on end can become offensive to the eye. Use bulletin boards to stimulate interest in forthcoming units of study. Put up new displays a day or two before a new unit is introduced.

SPECIAL BOARDS

1. Blind or Partially Sighted

Make boards touchable. Use different textures. Fabrics, such as; velvet, burlap, denim, seersucker, etc., could be used. Use sandpaper, corrugated paper, etc. By constantly maintaining a smooth background, the students will know what to look for on the board. The displays will be more prominent to the touch.

Glue several letters made of tagboard or sandpaper together so that they have depth. Make the letters, numbers, etc., extra large if the children are partially sighted.

Keep the boards low enough so that the students can feel them. Avoid the use of pins, tacks or other sharp objects.

Although the children are sight-impaired, do not neglect good taste and design. Both are most important. These children need to know what constitutes good design.

2. Physically Handicapped

Make the boards durable. The spastic child who knocks something off the board may shy away from bulletin boards in the future. Avoid having displays "stick out" in classrooms with the physically handicapped children. Keep boards low for children in wheelchairs. Avoid the use of tacks, pins or other sharp objects.

3. Learning Disabilities

Simplicity is important. Avoid cluttered boards. Relevancy is extremely important. Use block letters so students can relate to printed material. Do not use free-form or impressionistic lettering. (See lettering section.)

Be sure the boards are related to subject matter being studied at the time. To avoid confusing the child, a blank board would be better than old material facing the child when new material is presented or vice-versa.

For children with concentration problems, use subdued colors, such as the pastels. Avoid the use of excitable colors, such as; bright red, orange or any of the many fluorescent colors.

It might be wise to avoid the use of tacks, pins or other objects, such as fasteners lest the children remove them from the board.

MATERIALS

Save everything and anything! Be on the constant lookout for materials to use in your displays. Use new and unusual materials instead of the routine. Bulletin board materials should be used as one uses accessories to enhance a wardrobe. By getting away from the routine, a dramatic and interesting visual aid can be created.

1. Background

Most ideas in this book are routine since the author cannot anticipate what the teacher has at his/her disposal. Consequently, if a direction calls for a black background, substitute fabric or other material if available. Other different background materials besides construction paper are as follows:

A. Newspaper — especially the Sunday comic section.
B. Gift wrap.

C. Fabric. (Scraps make a nice patchwork effect. To make this durable, glue scraps onto heavy paper cut to size of board.)
D. Adhesive-backed paper.
E. Wallpaper.
F. Scrap paper. (Old assignment sheets, etc.)
G. Road maps.
H. Pages from brochures.
I. Spray paint.
J. Magazine covers and pages.
K. Plastic or plastic wrap over colored paper.
L. Waxed paper.
M. Aluminum foil.
N. Paper napkins or placemats. (Many restaurants use game-type mats and are usually willing to give you a few.)
O. Brown, white or store wrapping paper.
P. Grocery bags or other bags.
Q. Colored plastic garbage bags.
R. Old posters.
S. Carpet or rug samples.
T. Plastic or paper tablecloths.

2. Mat or Frame

If it is necessary to mat or frame your pictures, here are some materials you might use. Try combining some items to create unusual effects. Be careful, however, not to call more attention to the mat or frame and detract from the picture. Make the picture and surrounding material complement each other.

A. Paper doilies.
B. Gift wrap.
C. Old poster board.
D. Newspaper or magazine pages.
E. Aluminum foil.

F. Foam meat trays.
G. Foam egg cartons.
H. Pipe cleaner braids.
I. Straws.
J. Plastic tape.
K. Old neckties.

3. Special Effects

Save other materials for special effects. Keep a box to be filled with the "junk" you accumulate. Some of this "junk" could become very valuable as teaching aids. Valuable "junk" you might collect is in the following list.

A. Greeting cards and invitations.
B. Bridge tallies.
C. Packing materials-especially foam and paper straw.
D. Stationery pictures or emblems.
E. Unusual paper plates or cups.
F. Ribbon.
G. Gift tie.
H. Plastic flowers or fruit.
I. Playing cards.
J. Old magazines. Keep a file of pictures that you cut from magazines.
K. Picture negatives.
L. Anything that you think has possibilities.

SECTION II: "LANGUAGE ARTS"

Section II will give you help in preparing bulletin boards in these language arts areas; communications, listening, word recognition, prefixes, suffixes, grammar, library and dictionary skills.

1. VOWELS (Grades K-3)

A. Preparation and Materials: Staple a white background of your choice to the board.

Using red and white striped fabric, cut a scalloped canopy to fit across the top of the board. Cut out black block letters to spell the title. Cut one seal body and two flippers from black paper. Cut five circles for vowel letters, each one a different color. Cut block letters for vowels or print directly on the circles. Use a black button or gumdrop for the seal's nose.

B. Directions for Assembly: Staple the canopy across the top of the board and add the letters VOWELS to it. Beneath the canopy, place the vowel circles in an arc. Attach the seal body, flippers and nose under the vowel circles.

2. FEEL THE WORD (Grades K-2)

A. Preparation and Materials: Staple a background of bright green construction paper or other smooth material to the board. Cut block style letters from sandpaper to spell the title. Using the Dolch Basic Sight Word List, cut five or more words in block style also from sandpaper.

```
┌─────────────────────────┐
│  FEEL THE WORD          │
│                         │
│        CAT              │
│                         │
│        RAT              │
│                         │
│        FAT              │
│                         │
│        BAT              │
│                         │
│        SAT              │
└─────────────────────────┘
```

B. Directions for Assembly: Staple the title letters across the top of the board and the Dolch List Words in a column down the center of the board.

C. Variation: Cut out several alphabet sets from sandpaper and leave in a box near the board. Also, have 2 × 3 inch cards with sight words on them. Allow students to pick out a word and pin the letters to the board. Cut consonants from tagboard or other material and cut only vowels from sandpaper. Allow students to pin word letters to the board.

3. SIGHT WORDS (Grades K-2)

A. Preparation and Materials: Staple a brown or black background to the board. Cut block style title letters from white paper. Cut the clown parts out of any bright colors. For the head cut a white circle and draw on the face or cut the features from construction paper and glue on. Add yarn for hair. Use paper cupcake cups for ruffles at the neck, wrists and ankles. Cut several other white circles. Write Sight Words on these circles.

Sight Words

no was run saw the come yes

B. Directions for Assembly: Staple the title and the clown parts to the board. Add the ruffles and hat. Glue the Sight Word circles to the body of the clown.

4. ODD MAN OUT (Grades 1-5)

A. Preparation and Materials: Staple a background of any colored construction paper to the board. Cut letters to spell the title from magazines, using various shapes, colors and sizes. Prepare a variety of sheets (use medium weight paper so that it can be saved or else laminate it) on which five to ten stickmen have been drawn all alike except one. Some may be colored, minus a hat, uncolored or of a different color. Felt pen.

B. Directions for Assembly: Staple the title letters to the board and draw the stickmen in the upper right section of the board with the felt pen. Staple several of the prepared sheets to the board.

5. MAKE YOUR WORD GARDEN GROW (Grades 3-8)

A. Preparation and Materials: Staple a blue (sky) background on the top half of the board and a black (earth) background on the bottom half. Cut five carrots from orange material, five small and 15 large leaves (three for each carrot) from green material. Cut clouds in various shapes from white paper. Write the words from the illustration on the leaves, carrots and clouds with a felt pen.

B. Directions for Assembly: Glue three large leaves and one small leaf to each carrot and staple to the board so the carrots are in the black and the leaves in the blue. Staple the clouds to the sky area of the board.

C. Variation: The words used in this activity are compound. You could also use root words with prefixes or suffixes.

6. WHERE SHALL I LOOK? (Grades 4-8)

A. Preparation and Materials: Staple a black background to the board. Cut the title letters from magazines using different shapes and sizes. Select seven sheets of construction paper, each a different color. On the right-hand edge print with black felt pen from top to bottom the words TITLE PAGE, PREFACE, TABLE OF CONTENTS, TEXT, APPENDIX, GLOSSARYand INDEX, one title per sheet. On the left side of each sheet write the purpose of that book section. This should not show when the board is completely assembled. Write the word COVER across the bottom of an eighth sheet of paper. Cut a "Kilroy" face and two hands from white paper and add two black eyes to the face with felt pen.

B. Directions for Assembly: Attach the title letters at random to the top of the board.

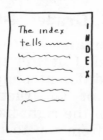

Staple the pages to the board, add each succeeding sheet so that only the letters on the right edge show. Staple these sheets on the left edge only. Add the "Kilroy" face and hands to the cover and attach cover to the board. Be careful not to staple any sections closed so the purposes can be read.

C. Variation: Use as a game. Ask the children questions about book sections. When they answer correctly, have them attach that section to the board.

D. Suggestions for Use: Show the sections and their uses of reference works as well as texts.

7. CRITICAL THINKING (Grades 4-8)

A. Preparation and Materials: Staple a black or brown background to the board. Cut white block letters to spell STAY ON THE RIGHT TRACK TO CRITICAL THINKING. Other materials needed are twine or clothesline for track and section crosspieces, 2 long pieces for the ovals and 22 short ones for the sections, chalk or white ink for lettering and fixative spray if chalk is used.

B. Directions for Assembly: Pin the long pieces of twine or clothesline to the board for the track and add the crosspieces to divide it into 22 sections. Pin the block letters to the center of the track. Print the following in every other space around the track using the ink or chalk: Be able to Draw Inferences, Recognize Paragraph Organization, Make Predictions, Summarize, Generalize, Draw Conclusions, Recognize the Author's Purpose, Interpret Figurative Language, Note Cause and Effect Relationships, Compare to Previous Readings, Relate Material to Own Experiences. If chalk is used, be sure to spray with fixative to prevent smearing.

C. Variations: 1. Instead of putting up all the sections at once, add a topic as you discuss it in the unit.

2. Add topics of your own that apply to the material you are using.

8. SQ3R = BETTER LEARNING (Grades 6-8)

A. Preparation and Materials: Staple a background of any light colored construction paper to the board. Cut block letters for the title and four arrows from paper that compliments the background color. Cut a sextant, question mark, book and lips from different colors of construction paper. Cut a rectangle from white paper. Write the word SURVEY on the base of the sextant, QUESTION on the question mark, READ on the spine of the book, RECITE on the lips and REVIEW on the rectangle.

SQ 3R = BETTER LEARNING

B. Directions for Assembly: Staple the title across the top of the board. Attach the objects to the board and add the arrows.

C. Possible Uses: Put this display up at the beginning of the school year when you will want to get your students started with good study habits. Use at other times for review.

9. NEWSPAPER SERVICES (Grades 5-8)

A. Preparation and Materials: Staple a white paper background to the board. Several sheets of newspaper and a felt pen are needed.

B. Directions for Assembly: Staple sheets of newspaper to the right side of the board. Beginning at the top, roll the newspaper diagonally, exposing the white paper, then secure the roll with tacks. Staple newspaper sheets to the left side of the board. Beginning at the bottom, roll the paper diagonally and secure the roll. Trim the ends so that they do not hang beyond the board. Staple newspaper sheets to the top and roll the paper parallel, then secure the roll. Repeat on the bottom with more newspaper. Print with the felt pen on the white paper the title THE FOUR SERVICES OF A NEWSPAPER. Add the following list below the title:

1. Information
2. Advice
3. Help
4. Entertainment

C. Suggestions for Use: Prepare this board when studying a journalism unit or use it in the student newspaper staff room.

10. WANT ADS (Grades 6-8)

A. Preparation and Materials: Staple a white background to the board. Cut a set of block letters from black paper to spell HOW TO READ THE WANT ADS. Cut another slightly smaller set of block letters also to spell the title from newspaper. One page of want ads from a newspaper, glue and a red felt pen are needed to complete this board.

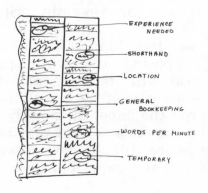

B. Directions for Assembly: Glue the smaller title letters onto the block title letters and staple them to the board. Tear the want ad sheet in half vertically and attach to the left side of the board. Circle abbreviations in the ads with a red felt pen continuing the line to the right side of the board. Print the complete word for the abbreviation opposite the line.

C. Suggestions for Use: Prepare this board as part of a journalism unit, a display in the student newspaper staff room or as a part of a careers class.

11. POTPOURRI (Grades K-8)

A. Preparation and Materials: Staple the want ad section of a newspaper to the board for a background. Cut out a free form piece of white construction paper and print POTPOURRI on it with red felt pen. Collect or have the children bring assorted items, such as; bubble gum cards, comics, limericks, poems, news oddities, riddles, pictures, etc., to cover the entire board.

B. Directions for Assembly: Staple the title shape to the top of the board. Attach collected items to the board adding something new each day. Remove the old items as new items are put up on display. Encourage the children to add items.

C. Variation: For kindergarten or first grade, this could be used as a reading readiness skill. In the older grades, use the board to display only articles pertaining to one subject which would appear in the title shape.

12. JIMINY CRICKET! (Grades 1-8)

A. Preparation and Materials: Staple a background of your choice to the board. Cut free form letters spelling the title from a color to

compliment the background. On a large piece of white paper draw the wall, write a joke, riddle or silly poem in each block and cut it out. Using green paper (felt is good if available), cut out the head and body parts for Jiminy Cricket. Cut a small circle of white paper for his eye and a smaller circle for the pupil out of black paper. Also from black paper cut a top hat, a pair of shoes, a cane and strips for the neck, arms and legs. The mouth, gloves and bow tie are to be cut from red paper.

B. Directions for Assembly: Staple the wall across the bottom of the board and the title letters across the top. Assemble the Cricket figure on the top of the wall.

C. Variations: 1. Instead of jokes, etc., on the wall blocks, write book titles appropriate for the age group in the room where the board is used. If possible, have those actual books on a low table beneath the board.

2. Change the word READING in the title to WRITING and use this board to spur interest in a creative writing lesson putting topics on the wall blocks.

13. GOOD SPELLING (Grades 3-8)

A. Preparation and Materials: Staple a paper background of any color to the board. You will need felt pens and/or crayons to complete this board.

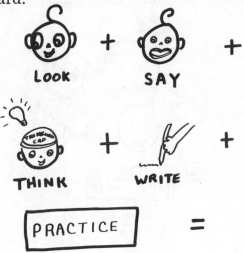

B. Directions for Assembly: All lettering and drawings are to be done directly on the background. Print the words and signs with black felt pen. Use colored felt pens or crayons to draw the pictures.

C. Suggestions for Use: Since good spelling is emphasized throughout the school year, this board could be used at anytime.

14. FOOLISH AND FUNNY (Grades 2-8)

A. Preparation and Materials: Staple a background of any color or material to the board. Cut three circles of various diameters for faces and six ears from yellow construction paper. Glue the ears to the faces and use a felt pen to draw features on the faces. Cut out several cartoons from newspapers and magazines. Write some funny sayings on white paper.

B. Directions for Assembly: Staple the faces to the upper left side of the board. Write the title with felt pen alongside the faces. Staple the cartoons, etc., to the bottom of the board.

C. Suggestions for Use: 1. Put this board up when studying a unit on humor; use it anytime and have children bring in their favorite cartoons.

2. To keep interest high, take down old cartoons and sayings and put new ones up everyday.

15. COMIC CAPER (Grades 3-8)

A. Preparation and Materials: Staple on the board a background of any color construction paper, newspaper, brown paper bags or wrapping paper. To letter the title, write directly on the background with a felt pen, use black yarn or cut letters from the comic section of the newspaper. Collect several Sunday comic strips from the newspaper cutting them apart into single pictures. You will also need glue and more black yarn to run the dividing line down the board.

B. Directions for Assembly: Write directly on the board or otherwise attach the title. Glue on the black yarn line continuing down from the title. Arrange the individual comics in random order within sections marked off by the yarn.

C. Suggestions for Use: Display this board when discussing story sequence sense.

16. SUPERSTITIONS (Grades 3-8)

A. Preparation and Materials: Staple an orange paper or fabric background to the board. Cut block letters to spell the title, a frame for the superstition list and a cat from black construction paper. On orange or white paper type or print a list of superstitions, e.g., garlic, when stuffed into keyholes, will prevent evil spirits from entering your house.

B. Directions for Assembly: Staple the title letters diagonally left to right to the board. Put the cat in the upper right side of the board and the list in the lower left side. Attach the frame around the list.

C. Variations: 1. Make several superstition lists and change them frequently.

2. Put up a blank sheet and let children add their own.

D. Suggestions for Use: This board could be used at Halloween time.

17. HOW WISE R U? (Grades 4-8)

A. Preparation and Materials: Staple a yellow or orange paper background to the board. Cut black free form letters to spell the title. To make the owl, cut an outline of the bird and two eye inserts from black paper. Cut the feet and beak from yellow paper and eyes from white paper. Print or type several brain teasers on 3 × 5 inch cards. Write the answers upside down or have the children ask you if their answers are correct. Glue these cards onto black paper and cut around the edges with pinking shears.

B. Directions for Assembly: Staple or pin lettering to the top of the board. Add the owl and arrange the cards at random on the rest of the board.

C. Suggestions for Use: This board would be appropriate not only for Halloween, but also during the year as a general interest board.

18. BREW UP AN INTEREST IN READING (Grades 3-8)

A. Preparation and Materials: Staple an orange background to the board. Cut black free form letters to spell the title. To make the witch, cut the body and the hat from black paper and the face and hand from green paper. Use shredded tissue paper or yarn for the hair. Cut the caldron from black paper leaving a cut out opening in the top. Cut the puffs of smoke from white paper. On each print one of the following topics: Adventure, Mysteries, Humor, Biographies, Fiction, Non-Fiction. Other materials you will need are torn paper scraps and cellophane for flames; a small stir stick, real or cut from paper, for the witch.

B. Directions for Assembly: Staple the lettering to the top of the board. Add the caldron, filling the opening with torn paper scraps, then crinkle colored cellophane and staple under the caldron for flames. Attach the smoke puffs above and the witch alongside the caldron. Glue the stick from the witch's hand to the caldron opening.

C. Suggestions for Use: This would be a good board to display during library week, book week or a book sales campaign.

—30—

19. A GOOD LISTENER (Grades 3-8)

A. Preparation and Materials: Staple a background (any color) of your choice to the board. Cut block letters to spell the title or write directly on the background with felt pen.

B. Directions for Assembly: If block title letters are used, staple them to the board. With a felt pen draw a large ear on the right side of the board. On the left side list the following

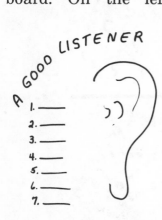

qualities of a good listener: 1. Has Good Posture 2. Disregards Distractions 3. Watches the Speaker 4. Thinks About What the Speaker is Saying 5. Relates What He Hears to What He Knows 6. Follows Sequences and Clue Words 7. Avoids Finding Fault With the Way the Speaker Is Speaking.

C. Variation: Change #3 on the list to Doesn't Talk to Others While On the Phone and this board could be used to teach good telephone listening habits.

20. HOW DO WE LISTEN? (Grades 3-8)

A. Preparation and Materials: Staple a background of your choice to the board. Cut block letters to spell the title and the four section topics from construction paper to blend with your background. Cut out several pictures of radios from magazines, catalogs, etc. Cut several question marks and ears from various colors of paper. Cut several sets of letters spelling REVIEW from colored paper, use magazine cutouts or write the word on pieces of colored paper. You will also need plastic tape or paper strips to mark off sections on the board and pins.

HOW DO WE LISTEN?

B. Directions for Assembly: Mark off a 6-8 inch space at the top of the board with plastic tape or paper strips. Pin the title letters in this area. Do not push pins completely into the board. Keep the letters at the head of the pin to give them more dimension. Divide the rest of the board using the tape or strips in the manner shown in the illustration. Attach the section titles the same way as the title letters. Staple the radio pictures in the TUNE IN section, the question marks in the QUESTION section, the ears in the LISTEN section and the words in the REVIEW section.

21. SPELLING SCRAMBLE (Grades 3-8)

A. Preparation and Materials: Staple a background of your choice in any color to the board. Cut block letters to correspond to the spelling unit number you are using for the scrambled words. You will also need colored construction paper cut in several free form shapes and a felt pen to write on the shapes scrambled spelling words.

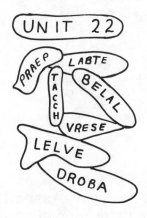

B. Directions for Assembly: Staple the title to the top of the board. Then staple in random order the pieces of paper with scrambled words on them.

C. Variation: Have some children assigned to scramble the letters and put up the board each week.

22. MONSTER OF THE DAY! (Grades 3-8)

A. Preparation and Materials: Staple a background of aluminum foil to the board. Cut free form or magazine letters to spell the title. Select children to draw the monster of the day (week) on a piece of paper to fit the size of the board. (Use volunteers or pull names from a hat.) Write a "demon" word on a smaller piece of paper.

B. Directions for Assembly: Attach the title letters and the monster to the board. Add the "demon" word to the monster.

23. DON'T BE SPOOKED! (Grades 3-8)

A. Preparation and Materials: Staple a black background to the board. Tear title letters from white paper. Tear white paper strips to form the house outline. Cut several ghost shapes from white paper and write a tricky spelling word on each one. You will also need white thread or string, glue and straight pins.

B. Directions for Assembly: Staple the title to the top of the board. Attach the house outline to the board. Make the cobwebs of white thread. Pin a piece of thread to the corner of the house. Bring the thread out to desired length for cobweb and cut. Pin the end to the board. Continue until the desired size of web is reach-

ed. Carefully glue ends in place and remove pins. Pin a piece of thread at the side for cross web-bing. Drape thread across lengthwise threads looping the threads and securing with glue. Cut the end of the thread and pin to board. Continue until the cross web-bing meets the end of the lengthwise threads. Attach the ghosts to the board anywhere inside the house.

C. Variations: 1. Instead of tricky spelling words, use words with irregular pronunciations.

2. In early grades use it to illustrate blends and digraphs.

24. PREFIXES (Grades 3-8)

A. Preparation and Materials: Staple a yellow fabric or construction paper background to the board. On two 1½ × 3 inch cards print prefixes. Fold several 3 × 5 inch cards in half lengthwise. Print words that go with each prefix on the front of a folded card. Also needed will be a felt pen for lettering, green florist wire to make figures and yarn. Twist pieces of the wire to form the figures in shapes shown in the illustration.

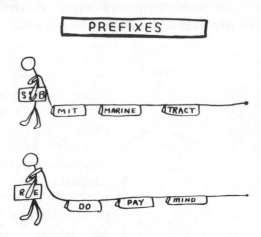

B. Directions for Assembly: Use the felt pen to letter the title directly on the board. Pin the wire figures to the board and attach a small prefix card under the hanging arm so it appears that he is carrying the sign. Attach the yarn to the bent arm. Let the yarn droop somewhat and attach near the opposite end of the board. Put the folded cards that match the prefix over the yarn.

C. Variations: 1. Change title to VERB FORMS and show irregular verbs in the present, past and participial forms.

2. Change title to SYLLABLES and show word divisions.

25. COMPOUND WORDS (Grades 2-8)

A. Preparation and Materials: Staple a background of your choice to the board. Cut block letters to spell the title from brown paper bags. Use lunch size paper bags to make puppets. Cut faces from colored paper and glue to the bags. Cut a bow tie for each puppet in a variety of colors. Print a compound word on each tie and glue to the puppet.

B. Directions for Assembly: Staple the title letters to the board and add the paper bag puppets.

C. Variations: 1. Change the title to SYLLABLES and show two syllable word divisions.

2. Change the title to PLURALS and show irregular plural forms.

3. Change title to VERB FORMS or SUFFIXES and illustrate them.

26. ANTONYMS ARE AN OPEN AND SHUT CASE (Grades 2-8)

A. Preparation and Materials: Staple a background of any colorful material (e.g., red burlap, denim, or construction paper) to the board. Cut a large rectangle of white paper and print the title on it. Glue a button to the right side to represent a door knob. Cut an even number of small squares from white paper. Have enough to fill the space available on your

board. Divide the squares into two piles. Take one pile and cut a door in the center of each square. Insert a brad for the door knob. Glue all but the door of each of these squares onto a plain square from the other pile. Print a word on the door and its antonym inside the door.

B. Directions for Assembly: Staple the title rectangle to the top of the board. Attach the doors in the area remaining on the board.

C. Variations: 1. Use this as a dictionary exercise. Have the children look up the word and write its antonym inside the door.

2. Have the children use a thesaurus to find as many antonyms as they can for the word that is given and write them in.

3. Change the title to PLURALS, COMPARATIVES or SYNONYMS and write an appropriate word inside the door.

27. HOMONYMS (Grades 3-8)

A. Preparation and Materials: Staple a background of your choice to the board. For title lettering cut magazine letters, block letters or print directly on the background with a felt pen. Select a variety of large two-holed buttons. Use blue ballhead pins for eyes and red self-stick coding dots for mouths or glue on red paper. Make stick bodies from pipe cleaners, one for each button. Cut derby hat shapes for half of the buttons and top hats for the rest. Print homonym pairs on the hats, such as; sale on the derby hat and sail on the top hat.

HOMONYMS

B. Directions for Assembly: Staple the title letters to the board or print them directly on it. Staple the pipe cleaner bodies in pairs to the board and add the buttons with the pins. Add the derby hats to the left heads and the top hats to the right heads. Put as many pairs as you have room for and can find homonyms.

C. Variation: Write homographs on the hats and have the children explain the differences, for example: bass — bass, bow — bow, lead — lead, etc.

TEACHER'S NOTE: Homographs must be spelled the same but may be pronounced differently.

28. DICTIONARY DAISIES (Grades 4-8)

A. Preparation and Materials: Staple a black background to the board using either a rough textured cloth, such as burlap or use construction paper. Cut letters spelling DIC-

TIONARY out of black paper in block style or use black plastic tape. Cut the top off a plastic container (bleach bottle) so the bottom is six inches tall. Cut the bottom in half making two half circles. Glue or tape the word DIC-TIONARY to the container. Decorate it further with colored tape. To make the flowers, cut 35 petals from one color or several colors of paper. Staple five petals together for one flower and glue a cotton ball on for the center. Cut seven strips of tagboard 1 inch wide and various lengths, at least 7 inches though. Print vertically with felt pen the following words on these stems: Definitions, Etymology, Pictures, Pronunciation, Spelling, Inflected Forms and Syllabication.

B. Directions for Assembly: Attach the plastic container to the board by inserting pins diagonally from the outside of the container. Insert the pins into the board at an angle from the bottom to hold the container upright. Staple or glue the flowers to the stem and put them in the container. If they do not stand properly, stuff some crumpled paper in the container to fill up the extra space.

29. MAIL CALL (Grades 1-2)

A. Preparation and Materials: Staple a green background of burlap or construction paper to the board. Cut white or black block letters to spell the ti-

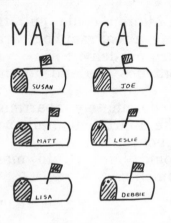

tle. Prepare a duplicating sheet with a mailbox and flag pattern on it and distribute to the children to be cut out and assembled. When the items are cut out, fold on A to close the flap. Children should attach the flag with a brad and color the flag. Use an adhesive at point B so the mailbox door can be opened and closed. Write their names in large letters on the boxes. Have the children write a sentence on a piece of paper, sign it and place it in their mailbox putting the flag up.

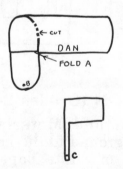

B. Directions for Assembly: Staple the title to the board. Staple the mailboxes to the board, but be careful not to staple the door or the flag because they must be movable. Remove the sentences from the mailboxes and place one of these sentences in each mailbox (don't give a child his own sentence). Make sure the mail flags are down.

C. Variations: 1. Children could pull the name of a classmate from a real mailbox, write a message to the person and deliver it.

2. Begin with one sentence and add another each day.

3. In an area of predominately apartment dwellers, you could make apartment mailboxes from large pieces of tagboard.

4. The mailboxes could be used to make classroom helper assignments.

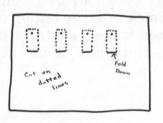

30. PUNCTUATION (Grades 2-8)

A. Preparation and Materials: Staple a colored paper background to the board. Cut five rectangular pieces of white paper. Make one shorter to use for the title. Use a felt pen matching the background color to print the title. Bend pipe cleaners to make the two stickmen on either side of the title. The remaining stickmen are to be drawn with a felt pen. Punch two holes at both ends of the four remaining rectangles.

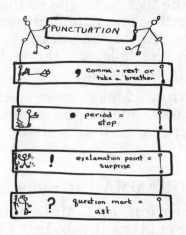

Letter them according to these diagrams. You will also need yarn or twine.

 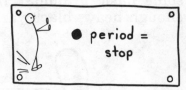

B. Directions for Assembly: Staple the title sheet to the board. Staple or pin the stickmen to the title rectangle so they appear to be holding up the sign. Attach the yarn or twine to the outside arm of the stickmen. Thread the yarn through the holes on the rectangles and staple them to the board.

C. Variation: Make more rectangles for quotation marks, apostrophe, colon, semicolon, dash and hyphen so that you can change the board.

31. GOOD GRAMMAR (Grades 3-8)

A. Preparation and Materials: Staple a white background to the board. Cut four rectangles of white paper. Draw staff lines on them with a felt pen and print the title. Collect five 45 rpm records. In the center of each, glue on a circle of paper upon which has been written some basic grammar rule. You will also need enough heavy black yarn for the treble clef sign.

B. Directions for Assembly: To make the treble clef sign draw an outline first on the board in pencil, then glue or pin the black yarn to the outline. Add the five records and the staff rectangles to complete the board.

32. MAKE A SENTENCE (Grades 3-8)

A. Preparation and Materials: Choose a background of colored paper, foil, shelf paper, wallpaper or paper tablecloth and staple it to the board. Select one of the following for title letters: magazine cutouts, free form letters from colored paper or aluminum foil block letters. Collect four empty food boxes (cake or pancake mixes, pudding, etc.). Cover these boxes with paper and write one of these subjects on

Make a Sentence

each box — CAPITAL LETTERS, SUBJECT, PREDICATE, PUNCTUATION. Cut a spoon and a mixing bowl from colored paper leaving a cutout in the bowl top to add the "ingredients." Shred some paper to put into the bowl and have some pouring from the boxes. You may also use plastic wrap, colored rice or puffed cereals to indicate something pouring from the boxes into the bowl. Cut a piece of white paper to fit in the bowl and write ONE IDEA on it.

B. Directions for Assembly: Staple the title letters across the bottom of the board. Staple or pin the bowl to the board. Squeeze the bowl a little from the sides so that the front stands away from the board. Adjust the back to lie flat. Pin the empty boxes above the bowl. Glue shredded paper in the bowl and add the ONE IDEA paper. Glue on the materials you have for what is pouring from the boxes. Put the spoon in the bowl. Decorate the bowl if you like.

33. PARAGRAPH WAGON (Grades 3-8)

A. Preparation and Materials: Staple a background of your choice to the board. For the

title lettering use magazine cutouts, block letters or print directly on the board with felt pen or crayon. Cut a rectangle from colored paper for the wagon body to correspond to background color. Print on this the words MAIN IDEA. Cut a handle and two circles for wheels. On each circle print SUPPORTING IDEA.

B. Directions for Assembly: Write or staple the title to the board. Attach the handle to the wagon and staple to the board. Add the wheels to the wagon.

34. PARTS OF SPEECH NAMES (Grades 5-8)

A. Preparation and Materials: Staple a background of your choice to the board. Cut red block letters to spell the title and parts of speech. Cut a derby hat from black paper large enough to glue on the title letters. Make the eyes from white paper. Cut blue or brown circles and glue to the eyes for pupils. Draw on eyelids and lashes. Cut a red circle for the nose. Cut a mouth and take out a section of the bottom lip.

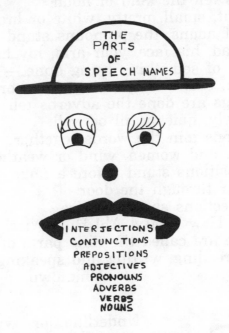

B. Directions for Assembly: Staple the hat and facial features to the board. When you staple the parts of speech to the board, position them so they look like the tongue.

35. PARTS OF SPEECH USES
(Grades 5-8)

A. Preparation and Materials: Staple a black background of paper, burlap or some other material to the board. On heavy white paper (watercolor weight paper is good because of the texture) write out the following verse:

"Three little words you often see
   are articles an, a and the.
A noun is the name of anything
   as school or garden, hoop or swing.
Adjectives tell the kind of noun
   as great, small, pretty, white or brown.
Instead of nouns, the pronouns stand —
   her head, his face, your arm, my hand.
Verbs tell of something being done —
   to read, count, laugh, sing, jump or run.
How things are done the adverbs tell —
   as slowly, quickly, ill or well.
Conjunctions join the words together
   as men and women, wind or weather.
The prepositions stand before a noun
   as in or through the door.
The interjections show surprise
   as Oh! How Pretty! Ah! How Wise!
The whole are called the nine parts of speech
   which reading, writing and speaking teach."
               —Unknown

Underline or write the parts of speech in a different color. Carefully burn around the edges of the paper. (Caution: Practice on scrap paper first because this must be done very quickly or the whole sheet will go up in flames.) Using a candle, touch the flame to the edge of the paper. With a cloth, quickly extinguish the flame leaving a seared edge.

B. Directions for Assembly: Staple the paper to the board.

36. HAIKU (Grades 4-8)

A. Preparation and Materials: Staple a shiny black background to the board. Cut one long and one short rectangle from rice paper. (Rice paper is available in art stores.) Any white paper may be used instead of the rice paper, but be sure to keep it flat after the ink lettering is added until it dries thoroughly. Use a brush and black drawing ink to letter the title on the shorter rectangle and to draw impressions of bamboo on the longer one. On white typing paper do some simple Japanese writing with the brush and ink. (Get samples of the writing from reference books on Japan.) Type students' Haiku poetry on these sheets.

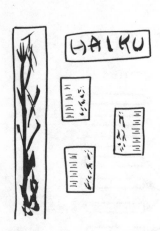

B. Directions for Assembly: Attach the long rectangle to the left side of the board and the title to the top. Arrange the Haiku sheets attractively on the rest of the board.

37. BOOKS WE READ (Grades 4-8)

A. Preparation and Materials: Staple any background to the board that will contrast with the yarn you will use. Cut block letters (your color choice) to spell the title BOOKS WE READ, AUTHORS and TITLES. On small pieces of paper type or print the name of authors of books your children have read. On an equal number of pieces of paper (same size as the author papers) type or print titles of books. To assemble this board you will also need pins and colored yarn.

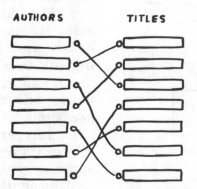

B. Directions for Assembly: Staple the title letters to the top of the board. On the top left attach the AUTHORS letters and on the right the TITLES letters. Under AUTHORS staple the author papers. Pin a piece of yarn on the right edge of these papers. Use different colors for each author. Under TITLES staple the title papers. On the left edge of these papers put pins for yarn. Match the authors and titles by correctly connecting the yarn to the empty pins.

C. Variations: 1. Students can work in pairs during free time to test themselves or each other.

2. Have the students make up the board using authors and titles from the classroom collection of books.

3. For upper grades, instead of authors and titles, use characters and quotations, etc.

38. THE WEB OF MYSTERY (Grades 3-8)

A. Preparation and Materials: Staple a black paper background to the board. For the spider web use white twine or thread, pins, glue

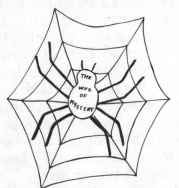

and a toothpick. Cut a large spider from white paper and use pipe cleaners for its legs. Letter the title, THE WEB OF MYSTERY, on the spider with black felt pen. For the other lettering you will need a pen and white ink.

B. Directions for Assembly: Using the white twine or thread, construct the spider web as shown. From the center point, bring out six strands of twine the same length and equal distance apart. Place a pin at one inch intervals along each strand. Connect the pins of each strand with twine until the web is the desired size. With toothpicks place glue under the twine to secure the web to the board. Remove all of the pins. Glue the pipe cleaners to the spider for legs and attach it to the board in the web. Between sections of the web write titles of good mysteries in white ink.

C. Variation: Instead of titles of mysteries to be read, write the names of good mystery shows on television.

39. SIGN IN PLEASE! (Grades 3-8)

A. Preparation and Materials: Staple a background of your choice to the board. Fold a

large piece of colored paper in half to resemble a book cover. (Desk blotter works well.) To the right side of the crease, punch two holes. Thread yarn or gift tie through them. Write SIGN IN PLEASE! on a sheet of paper and glue it to the left side of the crease. Cut several sheets of white paper to fit the right side of the book. Have the children write names of books, magazines, etc., that they have enjoyed. They can add a sentence or two about their reading to the sheet and sign their names. Punch these sheets to match the holes with the yarn.

B. Directions for Assembly: Staple the book cover to the board. As the children complete sheets about books they have read, tie the sheets to the right side of the cover.

C. Variations: 1. Have the children write about television programs or movies they have seen.

2. Have the children write about vacation trips they have taken.

40. THE LIBRARY WINDMILL OF MY MIND (Grades 4-8)

A. Preparation and Materials: Staple a sky blue background to the top two-thirds of the  board and a grass green background to the bottom one-third. Use felt pens directly on the board for any lettering. To make the windmill cut the base from white paper. Cut the roof from black paper the same width as the base and glue to the base. Make the door from red paper. Write on the door THE LIBRARY WINDMILL OF MY MIND and glue to the base. Use four pieces of heavy white paper to cut out the arms. On each, write one of the following: FICTION and NONFICTION, ATLASES, MAGAZINES, REFERENCE WORKS. Attach the arms to the mill with a brad. Cut a small fringe of green paper to show grass around the windmill. Cut seven large tulips with stems and leaves. Write one of the following on each tulip: ENCYCLOPEDIAS, VERTICAL FILE, READERS GUIDE, BIOGRAPHIES, CARD CATALOG, RECORDS, AUTOBIOGRAPHIES. Cut three free form white clouds.

B. Directions for Assembly: Staple the windmill to the board. Add the grass fringe in two segments on both sides of the windmill door. Staple the clouds in the sky area and the tulips across the bottom of the board.

41. THE CARD CATALOG (Grades 4-8)

A. Preparation and Materials: Staple a background of your choice to the board. The lettering can be done in any method you choose. Select an author card, a title card and a subject card from the card catalog. Reproduce each on a large piece of paper. You will need red, blue, green and other colored felt pens to label data on the board.

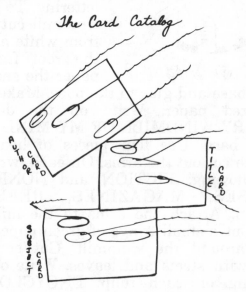

B. Directions for Assembly: If you cut title letters, staple them to the board. Otherwise, write directly on the background. Staple the three cards to the board and label them. With a blue felt pen circle the author on each card and label at the side. With red felt pen circle the title on each and label at the side. With a green felt pen, circle the subject on each and label at the side. With other colors, continue labeling the data on each card.

SECTION III: "SOCIAL STUDIES"

Section III will help you set up bulletin boards about your community, the United States (past and present), the world, government structures and geography.

1. COMMUNITY HELPERS (Grades K-3)

A. Preparation and Materials: Staple a community map or local newspaper to the board for the background.

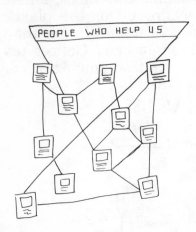

On a piece of heavy white paper print the title "People Who Help Us" with felt pen. Collect pictures of community helpers (postman, milkman, fireman, etc.,) and mat them with heavy white paper leaving extra space at the bottom to print the person's name and community position. Also needed is yarn or twine.

B. Directions for Assembly: Staple the title to the top of the board. Staple the pictures of community helpers randomly to the board. Connect the title to the pictures with yarn, twine or felt pen.

C. Variations: 1. Have students bring in the pictures (magazine pictures or their own artwork).

2. Take the children on a field trip (one day or several days). Take a camera along. For example, visit the fire station and take a picture of the fire chief or a fireman. Take pictures of fire fighting equipment. Construct a bulletin board on one kind of community helper and his/her services.

3. Depending on the area, you might include religious leaders, farmers, medical professionals, social workers, transportation personnel, etc.

2. TOOLS WE USE (Grades K-3)

A. Preparation and Materials: Staple a wood-like paper background to the board, or something of your choosing. Cut block letters compatible with the background or use plastic tape or felt pen. Cut the tool names larger than the names of the nail, screw, etc. Collect toy plastic tools, cut tool pictures from magazines or make sketches of them. Glue.

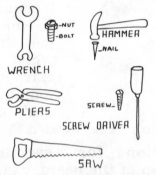

TOOLS WE USE

WRENCH

-NUT
-BOLT

HAMMER

-NAIL

PLIERS

SCREW-

SCREW DRIVER

SAW

B. Directions for Assembly: Put the title letters across the top of the board. Glue or staple the tools to the board and label them.

C. Variations: 1. Add pictures of people using these tools.

2. Find pictures (or sketch them) of older counterparts for these tools and do a bulletin board on TOOLS WE USED ONCE AND TOOLS WE USE NOW.

3. WHAT SHALL I BE? (Grades K-4)

A. Preparation and Materials: Staple a background of your choice to the board. Cut block letters to spell the title from any material compatible with the background. Cut a large question mark the height of the board from heavy paper. Cut out magazine pictures of people in various occupations.

Mat these pictures on circles of heavy paper in a color to match the background. (If preferred, cut rings from heavy paper instead of circles. Glue the pictures to the underside of the rings. This will give a picture frame effect and will add depth to the board.) Felt pen.

B. Directions for Assembly: Staple the large question mark to the board and attach the title letters. Attach the circles or frames to the question mark and label them with the felt pen.

4. TRANSPORTATION (Grades K-3)

A. Preparation and Materials: Staple a red background to the board. Cut the title letters

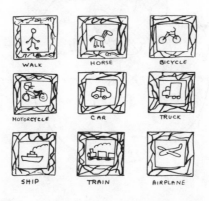

from a road map. Use the rest of the map to mat pictures of various means of transportation you have cut from magazines. Felt pen.

B. Directions for Assembly: Staple the title letters to the top of the board. Attach the matted transportation pictures to the board and label them with the felt pen.

5. OUR PLACE ON THE EARTH
(Grades 4-8)

A. Preparation and Materials: Staple a background of your choice to the board. Cut the title letters in a style and from a material of your choice. Cut a large circle for the world. Cut out a map of North America to fit proportionately within the world circle. With construction paper make an overlay of the United States in one color and your state in another color. Glue these onto the North America map. Felt pen.

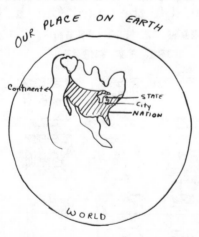

B. Directions for Assembly: Attach the world circle to the center of the board. Use the felt pen to label it WORLD. Staple the title letters to the board in an arc above the circle. Glue the North American Continent to the world circle in its right place. Label it with the felt pen. Label the United States, your own state and your city with the felt pen.

6. HANG IN THERE (Grades 4-8)

A. Preparation and Materials: Staple a background of your choice to the board. Cut a

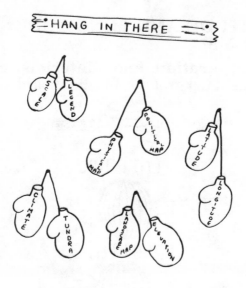

piece of brown paper long enough for the title. Use a felt pen or crayon to make it look like a board. Cut block letters for the title out of black construction paper and glue them on the paper "board." Cut out five hand size pairs of boxing gloves from brown paper. On each glove write a geographical term, such as; Latitude, Elevation, Climate, etc., with a felt pen. Connect the gloves in pairs with shoe laces. Pins.

B. Directions for Assembly: Attach the title with pins across the top of the board. Then attach the pairs of gloves randomly on the rest of the board with pins. Be sure that the writing side of the gloves is visible if the geographical term appears only on one side. Otherwise, you could write the terms on both sides of each glove.

7. LATITUDE AND LONGITUDE
(Grades 5-8)

A. Preparation and Materials: Staple a dark blue background to the board. Cut the

LATITUDE + LONGITUDE = GRID

letters under each circle from light blue construction paper in block style. Cut three large circles representing the earth from light blue construction paper as well as the nine arrows.

Using a dark blue felt pen divide one circle into latitude lines. Make the Equator line heavier. Divide the second circle into longitude lines. Make the Prime Meridian and International Dateline heavier. Divide the third circle into latitude **and** longitude lines. Again make the Equator, Prime Meridian and International Dateline heavier than the other lines. Write one of the following terms on each of the nine arrows: 0° Latitude, Equator, International Dateline, 180° Longitude, Prime Meridian, 0° Longitude, 180° Longitude, 0° Longitude and 0° Latitude. See the illustration for the direction of the arrows. Write the terms accordingly.

B. Directions for Assembly: Staple the latitude circle near the top of the board. Point the 0° Latitude arrow at the left edge of the Equator line and the Equator arrow at the right edge. Attach the **Latitude** block letters beneath this circle.

Staple the longitude circle to the center of the board. Add the International Dateline arrow and one 180° Longitude pointing to that line on the left. Add the Prime Meridian and one 0° Longitude arrow pointing to that line on the right. Attach the **Longitude** block letters beneath this circle.

Staple the third earth circle in the remaining board area. Staple the other 180° Longitude arrow pointing to the International Dateline on the left, the other 0° Longitude arrow pointing to the Prime Meridian on the right and the 0° Latitude arrow pointing to the Equator. Attach the **Latitude** + **Longitude** = **Grid** block letters beneath this bottom circle.

8. THE UNITED STATES (Grades 3-8)

A. Preparation and Materials: Staple a blue background to the board. Cut block letters to spell the title from dark blue, red and white construction paper, a complete title from each color. Draw a map of the United States directly on the board. (Use an opaque projector if necessary and one is available.) Be sure to include all the state boundaries plus the Great Lakes. Have each child choose one or two states (depending on the size of the class) and trace the state outlines from the map on the board. The child then makes a copy of the state on colored paper and adds the name of the state and its capital. Glue.

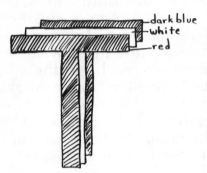

dark blue
white
red

B. Directions for Assembly: Pin the dark blue title letters to the top of the board to be sure the spacing is correct; then staple into place. Overlap the white title letters onto the blue leaving an edge of blue showing. Staple into place. Overlap the red title letters onto the white leaving an edge of white showing. Staple into place.

Have the children glue their states to the proper place on the United States map on the board.

C. Variations: 1. Add the U.S. flag, seal, motto, etc., to the board.

2. Have each child add the flag, seal, motto, etc., for his state on the board if there is room.

3. Use this as a products map. Have the children add cutouts of the state's chief products to the map.

4. To illustrate time zones, make states in each zone one color.

9. INDIANS OF NORTH AMERICA
(Grades 3-8)

A. Preparation and Materials: Staple a blue background to the board. Cut title letters  from foam egg cartons or foam fruit and meat trays. Determine how many tribes you want to display and cut that number of feathers from the foam materials. Fringe the edges to look like feathers. With a pencil, press a line down the center of the feather. Do not push the pencil all the way through. Bend the feather back slightly at the line. Cut strips of paper to fit the bottom half of each feather. Write the tribe names on these strips and glue them to the feathers. Cut the headband from foam egg carton cups. Separate the cups. Slit one side of the cup and cut out the bottom. Trim off the edges. Bend the cup so it is fairly flat and with scissors cut fringe into the top. Make as many as are needed to cover the end of the feathers. Cut three small feathers from a colored egg carton for the bottom of the headdress. Make another feather trim to cover these three feathers.

—65—

B. Directions for Assembly: Attach the large feathers to the board in the shape of an Indian headdress. Add the feather trims to cover the feather ends. Put the three smaller feathers at the base of the headdress pointing down. Attach the remaining feather trim to cover the ends of these three feathers. Add the title letters to the top of the board using the curvature of the feathers as a guide.

C. Variations: 1. Use paper for all the headdress parts rather than foam.

2. Use the board to display vocabulary for other subject areas.

10. SECRETS OF PLYMOUTH ROCK (Grades 3-8)

A. Preparation and Materials: Staple a background of your choice to the board,

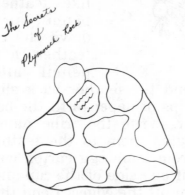

however, do not use black or gray. Cut a large rock from black or gray heavy paper. Divide the rock into sections and cut around three sides of these sections. Fold back the fourth side to act as a door hinge. Glue the rock to white paper being careful not to glue the "doors" to the white paper. Trim around outer edge of rock to get rid of excess white paper. Under each door write an important fact of this time period, such as; location of Plymouth Rock, who or how many landed there, year, etc. Felt pen.

B. Directions for Assembly: Attach the rock to the board. Letter the title directly on the board with felt pen. Be sure that the "doors" can open when the board is complete.

11. EARLY COLONIAL LIFE (Grades 3-8)

A. Preparation and Materials: Staple a background of your choice to the board. Glue

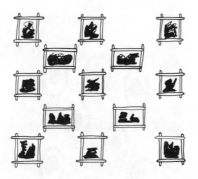

toothpicks together to spell the title. To preserve for the future, glue the letters onto heavy paper so that removal from the board will not ruin the letters. Cut out pictures of colonial life from old books and magazines or make some sketches and trim them to fit frames made of popsicle sticks. Glue the pictures onto the underside of the frames.

B. Directions for Assembly: Attach the lettering across the top of the board. Add the framed pictures on the remaining board area.

12. PORTRAITS OF LIBERTY
(Grades 3-8)

A. Preparation and Materials: Staple a white background to the board. Cut black block letters to spell the title. Cut a large Liberty Bell from gray or blue-gray paper. Draw the crack in the bell and other details with felt pen. Cut eight black paper silhouettes of revolutionary patriots. (They do not have to be exact outlines of the persons represented.) Cut ovals of white paper on which to mount the silhouettes. Cut black oval frames and glue on the matted silhouettes. Felt pen.

PORTRAITS OF LIBERTY

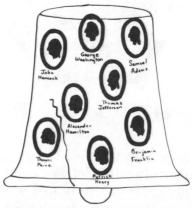

B. Directions for Assembly: Staple the title letters to the top of the board. Attach the

Liberty Bell centered beneath the title. Glue the framed pictures to the bell and print each patriot's name beneath his picture.

13. PRESIDENTS (Grades 3-8)

A. Preparation and Materials: Staple a background of your choice to the board. Type or

print a chronological list of Presidents of the United States on a piece of white paper. On smaller strips of paper print clues about each President. You may need as many as five clues for each name. Felt pen.

B. Directions for Assembly: Print the title directly on the top of the board. On the left side of the board write the word PRESIDENTS then, staple the list of Presidents under it. On the right side of the board write the word CLUES and number from 1 to 5 (space to fill the area opposite the Presidential list). Add a clue a day (maximum of five) about a President. Let the children have a contest to see who can guess the mystery President of the week. Cross out or cover the names as they are guessed.

14. REVOLTIN' REASONS (Grades 4-8)

A. Preparation and Materials: Staple a background of your choice to the board. Cut a rectangle of white paper and print the title on it with felt pen. Then cut rectangles to print the causes of the Revolutionary War, one cause on each strip. Punch two holes, one above the other, in each end of the cause rectangles. Punch one hole in the title rectangle on each side at the bottom. You will also need twine or yarn to thread the strips together.

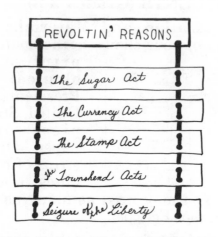

B. Directions for Assembly: Using the twine or yarn, thread the title and the cause rectangles together. Space them evenly to fill the board. Staple to the board.

C. Variation: Use this board to illustrate causes of other wars.

15. THE CIVIL WAR (Grades 4-8)

A. Preparation and Materials: Divide the board in half. Staple a blue background on the left side and a gray background on the right. Staple a white strip across the top and down the middle for the lettering. Cut the title letters in block style alternately from blue and gray construction paper. Cut blue block letters to spell THE BLUE and gray block letters to spell THE

GRAY. Make posters of white paper to tell the leaders, states, battles, etc., half pertaining to one side and half to the other. Carefully burn around the edges of these posters. (Caution: Practice on scrap paper first. This must be done very quickly or the whole sheet will go up in flames. Using a candle, touch the flame to the edge of the paper. With a cloth quickly extinguish the flame leaving a seared edge.)

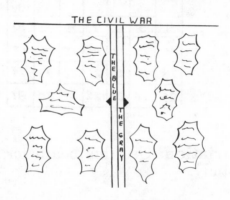

B. Directions for Assembly: Staple the title letters in the white strip at the top of the board. Staple the letters to the center strip vertically, THE BLUE on the upper left and THE GRAY on the lower right.

16. WORLD WARS (Grades 4-8)

A. Preparation and Materials: Staple a background of your choice to the board. Find a calendar for a war year or use any calendar and change the year to correspond to a war year. Write what happened on that particular day in each day square on the calendar. Felt pen.

B. Directions for Assembly: Staple the calendar to the board and use the felt pen to write the title directly on the board. This title could be the name of a war being studied.

Title						
Year						
Month						
Sun	Mon	Tue	Wed	Thur	Fri	Sat
				1	2	3
4	5	6	7	8	9	10
11	12	13	14	15	16	17
18	19	20	21	22	23	24
25	26	27	28	29	30	31

C. Variation: Use this board for any time-related study.

17. WARTIME (Grades 4-8)

A. Preparation and Materials: Staple a background of your choice to the board. Cut out

a large circle of heavy paper to represent a clock. Cut out twelve smaller circles from a contrasting color to represent the numbers. On each of these circles write a historical event of the war. Cut out two hands for the clock from black paper. Cut title letters from a material and style of your choosing. Felt pen.

B. Directions for Assembly: Staple the title letters to the top of the board or print them directly on the board. Attach the clock and glue the event circles in the number places. Be sure they are in sequential order. Attach the hands to the clock face in such a way that they can be moved to point to the circles. At the bottom of the board use the felt pen to write the name and dates of the war whose events appear in the circles.

C. Variation: Write the war and dates on separate pieces of paper so they can be changed to another war; if the war event circles are pinned to the clock, they can be changed. Have several sets of events belonging to several wars available; use this to survey wars throughout history, not just the wars the United States was involved in.

18. WHO STEPPED WHERE (Grades 3-8)

A. Preparation and Materials: Staple a background of your choice to the board. Cut the title letters from a material and in a style of your choice. Obtain a large map of the United States. Be sure to include Alaska and Hawaii. You may want to trim away everything but land areas. Cut several footprints and on each write the name of an explorer or person who contributed to a particular state's history. Felt pen.

B. Directions for Assembly: Staple the title letters to the top of the board or letter directly on the background with a felt pen. Put up the United States map with Alaska and Hawaii and add the footprints where they belong. If possible, save the map to use again.

C. Variation: Make the footprints smaller and in a different color for each explorer. Attach them to the map along the trails or in territories where these people made history. At the bottom of the board have a legend to identify the people belonging to the footprints.

19. OUR GOVERNMENT (Grades 5-8)

A. Preparation and Materials: Staple a background of your choice to the board. Cut black block letters to spell the title and glue them on a large tagboard rectangle. Cut rectangles of various sizes from white paper and write one of the following on each: Executive Branch, Legislative Branch, Judicial Branch, The President and Vice-President, Cabinet, The Senate, The House of Representatives, The Supreme Court, and The Lower Courts. Yarn or twine and glue are also needed.

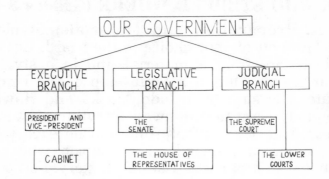

B. Directions for Assembly: Staple the title rectangle to the top of the board. Attach the remaining rectangles. Glue twine or yarn between the rectangles to join them together.

C. Variation: Use a different color for each government branch and the parts attached to it. For example, use red for all the Executive Branch, blue for all the parts of the Judicial Branch and white for the parts of the Legislative Branch.

20. CAPITAL CITIES (Grades 4-8)

A. Preparation and Materials: Staple a background of your choice to the board. Cut letters to spell the title from a material of your choice in either block or free form style. Cut squares of white paper and write the symbols given at the end of the directions for this bulletin board on them, one symbol on each square. Be sure to also write the alphabet letter on the square. Cut rectangles of white paper and using the symbols write the names of capital cities of the world or the United States on them. Cut squares to be used as pockets to hold paper strips. Cut lots of paper strips to fit in the pockets. You will need one pocket square for each capital city on the board. Felt pen. Small envelopes one for each capital city on the board.

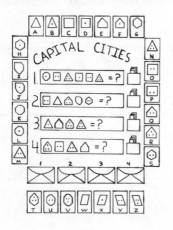

B. Directions for Assembly: Staple the symbol squares around the edge of the board to form a border. Staple the title letters in an arc near the top of the board. Pin city name papers to the board so they can be easily changed. Don't use too many at a time and be sure to change them often. Number them directly on the board with the felt pen. Staple a pocket square for each name to the right of that name and insert several paper strips in each pocket. Below the city name papers, number and staple as many envelopes as there are names. Do not staple the envelopes shut. Have children write the solution to each city on a strip of paper and sign it. They should put these strips in the envelope at the bottom of the board with the same number as the city.

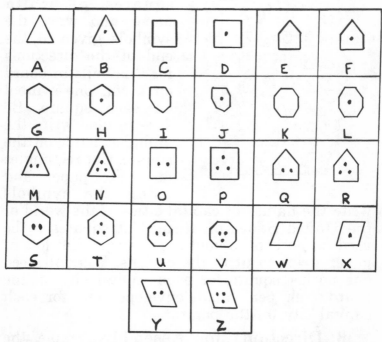

C. Variation: Have the children write the country or state for the capital city on the strip of paper, sign their names and insert into the envelopes.

21. AROUND THE WORLD (Grades 4-8)

A. Preparation and Materials: Staple a blue background to the board. Print the title on

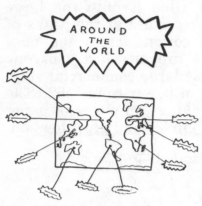

a piece of white paper and cut around the edge with pinking shears. Obtain a large map of the world. Cut out small pieces of paper with pinking shears. Print the name of a country on each. String or yarn and red self-stick coding dots are also needed.

B. Directions for Assembly: Pin or staple the title to the board. Beneath it staple the map. Attach pieces of string or yarn to countries on the map with red dots. Attach the other end of the string to the name of the country stapled outside the map.

C. Variations: 1. Have the children write to various embassies for information. When they receive a reply, cover the red coding dot with a blue one.

2. Have the children write to various state capitals for information. Change the coding dot color when it is received.

3. Beneath the country name write the mileage from your area to there.

22. ROYALTY (Grades 5-8)

A. Preparation and Materials: Staple a black background to the board. Cut block style letters from gold foil to spell FRENCH KINGS, HOUSE OF BOURBON and 1562-1830. Cut one large gold foil crown and one smaller one. The smaller crown needs to be as wide as the larger one but not as high. Glue it onto the large crown. Glue small colored stars at the peaks of the small crown and cotton across the base where the two crowns are attached. Cut one colored foil circle (or use large commercial stars or seals) for each king in power from 1562-1830. Write the names of the kings on pieces of paper that will fit on the foil circles and glue them on.

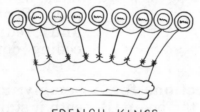

FRENCH KINGS
HOUSE OF BOURBON
1562 - 1830

B. Directions for Assembly: Attach the crown as assembled thus far to the board. Staple the colored foil circles with the names of the kings to the peaks of the whole crown. Staple the lettering beneath the crown.

23. PEOPLE AND PLACES (Grades 3-8)

A. Preparation and Materials: Staple any solid colored paper to the board for a background. (Caution: Do not use fabric. It will tend to pull and get "lumpy" as the children connect the dots.) Cut letters in any style and any material to spell the title or letter directly on the board. Make several "connect the dots" pictures using pictures from magazines, books, etc., for patterns (or buy a coloring book of people and places around the world). Laminate the dot pictures or make duplicated sheets of them. Grease pencils.

B. Directions for Assembly: Staple the title letters to the board or letter directly on it. Attach the dot pictures and add a grease pencil on a string to the board. Let the children connect the dots with the grease pencil during their free time.

24. COLLAGE (Grades 3-8)

A. Preparation and Materials: No background is needed other than a bulletin board itself. If lettering is needed, choose what would be appropriate for the topic that is selected. Suggest a topic to the children (current events, ecology, etc.). Have the children bring in magazine pictures or draw something that is representative of that topic.

B. Directions for Assembly: If any letters are used, staple them to the board. Staple the pictures onto the board forming a collage.

25. LIGHT UP A FACT (Grades 3-8)

A. Preparation and Materials: Staple an aluminum foil background to the board. Be sure that this board faces the light or a window. Cut the title letters from a material and in a style of your choice. Obtain a square box and cut the back out leaving one inch on each side with which to attach the box to the board. Cut a slit in the top of the box. Cut about one inch of paper tube (waxed paper, paper towel, etc.). Cut a circle in the front of the square box to fit the diameter of the tube. Put the tube in the hole. Cover the inside of the box with aluminum foil, shiny side out. Type an important fact on a card that will fit the slit in the top of the box. A small penlite flashlight, tape and staples are also needed.

B. Directions for Assembly: Tape the penlite flashlight to the back of the box making sure the switch is exposed for the children to turn on. Attach the box to the board. Use enough staples so it is very secure. Put a card in the slit on top. Have the children turn on the light and look through the tube at the fact in the box.

C. Variation: Have a small box of fact cards attached to the board so the children can put them in the slit and light them up.

SECTION IV: "MATH"

Section IV will help you display math skills of computation, equivalents, ratios, money, time, measurement, metric system, geometry and area.

1. ADD THE DOMINOES (Grades K-3)

A. Preparation and Materials: Staple a white background to the board. Cut black block letters to spell the title. Obtain a set of dominoes or cut a set out of black paper and add the dots with white ink. Felt pen and large pins.

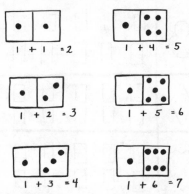

ADD THE DOMINOES

1 + 1 = 2
1 + 4 = 5
1 + 2 = 3
1 + 5 = 6
1 + 3 = 4
1 + 6 = 7

B. Directions for Assembly: Staple the title letters to the top of the board. Attach real dominoes to the board with the large pins, two pins above and two below. Use as many dominoes or combinations of dominoes as desired. Below the dominoes write numbers with felt pen. If you use paper dominoes, staple them on the board.

C. Variation: The dominoes may also be used for multiplication.

2. COUNTING (Grades K-3)

A. Preparation and Materials: Divide the board into four sections horizontally making the top section larger than the others for attaching the title letters. Staple a red background to the first and fourth sections and a black background to the second and third sections. Cut black block style letters to spell the title. Cut the club and spade suit symbols from black paper and the diamond and heart symbols from red. Numbered playing cards (not face cards) and black plastic tape or paper strips are also needed.

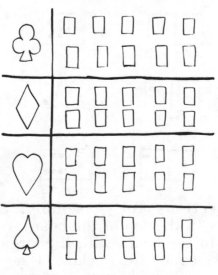

COUNTING

B. Directions for Assembly: Use the plastic tape or paper strips to divide the board into sections as shown in the illustration. Staple the title letters across the top of the first section and the suit symbols in the sections on the left. In each section staple cards from Ace to 10 of the same suit as the symbol.

C. Variation: Keep the clubs and hearts as in the basic board. Label the diamond symbol EVEN. Staple only even numbered cards to the board in this section. Label the spade symbol ODD. Staple only odd numbered cards to it.

3. NUMBER FOLKS (Grades 1-8)

A. Preparation and Materials: Staple a background of your choice to the board. Use individual sheets of paper or draw all the number figures on one sheet of tagboard. Cut around the board with pinking shears. Felt pen.

B. Directions for Assembly: Use the felt pen to write the title on the center of the board and outline it with a simulated pinked edge. Draw the number figures on individual sheets of paper with the felt pen and staple to the board. Make sure the numbers themselves are darker so they stand out. If you are using tagboard, draw the number figures on and staple to the board. Write the title in the center, drawing a simulated pinked edge around it.

4. PLACE VALUE (Grades 3-8)

A. Preparation and Materials: Staple a background of your choice to the board. Cut white block letters to spell the title. Cut six strips of white paper graduated in length. Cut six more strips of white paper graduated in length but shorter than the other set. Cut one long strip to fit across the bottom of the board. Use white tape or cut more white strips to make a triangle. Felt pen and pins.

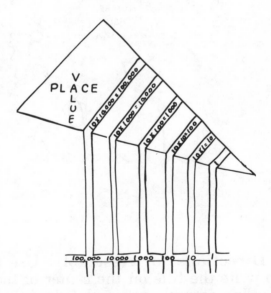

B. Directions for Assembly: With the felt pen on the SHORTER SET of six white strips write these numbers, one on each with the longest number equation on the longest strip,

10 × 10,000 = 100,000, 10 × 1,000 = 10,000, 10 × 100 = 1,000, 10 × 10 = 100, 10 × 1 = 10 and 1. Take the LONGER SET of six strips and pin them vertically to the board with the longest strip on the left and the shortest on the right. Pin the single long strip across these vertical strips near their bases. At each intersection from left to right write these numbers with the felt pen 100,000, 10,000, 1,000, 100, 10 and 1. At the tops of these vertical strips pin the numbered strips diagonally, longest on the top of the longest vertical strip, etc. Staple all the strips when you have them arranged. Remove the pins and trim away any ends that need it. Staple the title letters to the left of the longest diagonal. Use the tape or remaining strips to make a triangle around the title and top place value numbers.

5. MAYAN NUMBERS (Grades 4-8)

A. Preparation and Materials: Staple a background of your choice to the board. Cut title letters in a style of your choice or letter directly on the board with felt pen. Cut 20 small circles of one color, seven bars of another color and one oval of a third. Use the felt pen to add the markings to the oval shape. Felt pen.

B. Directions for Assembly: Staple or write the title on the board. Staple the figures to the board in two columns, zero to five on the left and six to ten on the right. The oval equals zero, one circle for one, two circles for two, a bar for five, circle over a bar for six and two bars for ten, etc. Add the equal signs and numbers with felt pen.

MAYAN NUMBERS

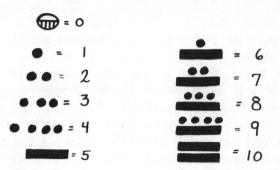

6. ROMAN NUMERALS (Grades 1-8)

A. Preparation and Materials: Staple a background of your choice to the board. Cut the title letters from black paper in block or Roman style. Cut the roof, columns and base of the building from white paper. Felt pen.

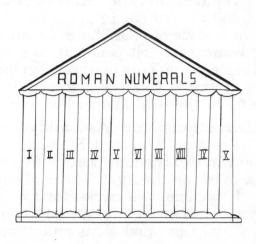

B. Directions for Assembly: Staple the building parts to the board. Add the title letters to the roof section and write the Roman numerals, one on each column, with the felt pen.

7. BIG AND LITTLE (Grades K-2)

A. Preparation and Materials: Staple a background of your choice to the board. Cut the title letters in a style and material of your choice or letter directly on the board with a felt pen. Collect pictures of objects in duplicate making sure one is large and the other small, e.g., a lion and a lion cub.

B. Directions for Assembly: Staple the letters to the board or write them on with felt pen with BIG on the left and LITTLE on the right. Staple the large objects on the left and the small objects opposite their counterparts on the right.

8. WHAT DO YOU MEAN? (Grades 2-8)

A. Preparation and Materials: Staple a background of your choice to the board. Cut free form letters to spell the title from a color compatible with the background. Cut several free form pieces of paper. Use a different color for each one. On each, write a math symbol and its definition with an example.

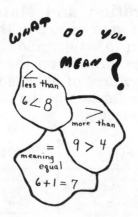

B. Directions for Assembly: Staple the title to the board. Staple the symbol forms to the board making sure that they all touch each other.

9. SETS (Grades 1-8)

A. Preparation and Materials: Staple a black or a bright colored paper to the board for the background. Cut white block letters to spell SETS. Then cut enough strips of white paper one inch wide to make the triangle and title section and enough white circles to fill the triangle. Collect pictures of sets of objects or draw them directly on the circles with crayons or felt pens. Pins.

B. Directions for Assembly: Staple the white strips on the board to form the triangle and title section. Add the title letters. Fill the triangle with the circle sets. If you pin the circles in the triangle, you can change them more easily.

C. Variations: 1. Cut out comic strip characters or faces from juvenile card games. Match them in sets; use this board as a basis for a classroom game.

2. Have a duplicate set of circles and have the children take turns going to the board to match the sets.

10. GROCERY SHOPPING (Grades 2-8)

A. Preparation and Materials: Staple a brown wrapping paper background to the board. Draw the dimensional shelving, centered on the board, with pencil first. Draw in two faint vertical lines for the back and the front of the cabinet and horizontal lines for the shelves. Add lines for the shelf width and depth. Go over

GROCERY SHOPPING

these lines with a felt pen. Collect labels from canned foods. Be careful to keep them flat and not creased anywhere. Write prices to go with the labels on small pieces of paper. Glue.

B. Directions for Assembly: Print the title across the top of the board directly on it with felt pen. Hold the labels as if they were still on the cans and staple the backs closed. Then staple them to the board inside the labels so they appear to be rounded and give a three-dimensional effect, as if they were sitting on the grocery shelves. Staple or glue the price labels to shelf "fronts" under the cans they apply to.

C. Variations: 1. This board can be used for classroom math. For addition and division use different sized labels to determine which would be cheaper, etc.

2. Use this board for nutrition or phonics.

11. TIME TABLES (Grades 2-6)

A. Preparation and Materials: Staple a background of your choice to the board. Write the times tables for numbers from two to ten in a vertical column on large pieces of heavy paper, one table on each piece. Make an animal strip for each times table out of tagboard. Pins and felt pen.

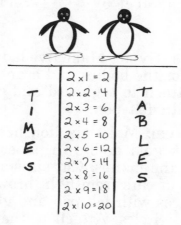

T I M E S   TABLES

$2 \times 1 = 2$
$2 \times 2 = 4$
$2 \times 3 = 6$
$2 \times 4 = 8$
$2 \times 5 = 10$
$2 \times 6 = 12$
$2 \times 7 = 14$
$2 \times 8 = 16$
$2 \times 9 = 18$
$2 \times 10 = 20$

Penguins (twos): Make two penguins. Use black paper for the body, head and flippers. Use white paper for the breast. Use yellow paper for the feet. Assemble on tagboard and draw the face on with felt pen.

Seagulls (threes): Cut three seagulls from white paper. Draw on eyes and beaks with felt pen. Attach to tagboard and outline with felt pen.

Snails (fours): Make four snails of white or yellow paper. Use hairpins or pipe cleaners for antennae. Add the detail lines with felt pen. Attach to tagboard. Outline with felt pen if necessary.

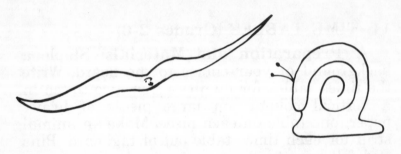

Seagulls (cut 3)   Snails (cut 4)

Lady bugs (fives): Make five lady bugs. Use black paper for the bodies and orange paper for the wings. Attach to tagboard and draw on the black dots with felt pen.

Lions (sixes): Make six lion heads. Cut six circles of dark gold or brown paper and fringe the edges for the manes. Cut six smaller circles and six pairs of ears from light brown or yellow paper, add faces with felt pen and glue onto the larger fringed circles. Attach to the tagboard.

Lady bugs (cut 5)   Lions (cut 6)

Cats (sevens): Make seven cats out of black or white paper. Cut tails for each from a contrasting color. Glue short pieces of broom straws to the underside of the head for whiskers. Attach to tagboard. Outline or add detail lines with felt pen.

Octopi (eights): Make eight octopus bodies of any color. Cut eight strips of paper for the legs of each octopus, pleat them and attach onto the back side of the body. Cut hats and glue on small plastic flowers. Attach to tagboard. Add funny faces with felt pen.

Cats (cut 7)   Octopi (cut 8)

Puppies (nines): Make nine puppies from brown wrapping paper. Cut each ear from a contrasting color and glue on. Draw the faces and tongues on with felt pen or cut out of colored paper. Attach to tagboard.

Bunnies (tens): Make ten bunnies out of white paper. Add cotton balls for tails. Attach to tagboard. Add any detail lines with felt pen.

Puppies (cut 9)   Bunnies (cut 10)

B. Directions for Assembly: Pin the times table to the center section of the board. Pin the matching animal heading to the top of the board. Change the times tables and animal headings each week or as often as desired. Print the title letters vertically in the two outside lower sections with felt pen.

12. DIVISION TALK (Grades 2-8)

A. Preparation and Materials: Staple a yellow background to the board. Make four arrows (one wide and three narrow) from black paper. Chalk, white crayons or white ink for lettering on black arrows. If you use chalk, be sure to spray with a fixative to prevent smearing. Felt pen.

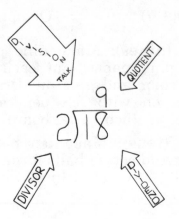

B. Directions for Assembly: Draw the division problem in the center of the board. Pin the three narrow arrows to the board with each one pointing to a different portion of the division problem, the quotient, the divisor and the dividend. Write these terms on the appropriate arrow Add the wide arrow in the upper left corner pointing to the problem. Write the title on this arrow.

13. FRACTIONS (Grades 3-8)

A. Preparation and Materials: Staple a background of your choice to the board making each section a different color (see illustration). Separate the sections with strips of plastic tape or colored paper. Cut out three circles, one for each board section and color in the appropriate fractional areas. Make aluminum foil rubbings of a quarter and half dollar. Trim around edges so they resemble actual coins. Obtain one play paper dollar, a set of measuring spoons and three empty (and washed out) milk cartons one quart, one half gallon, one gallon. Felt pen and more plastic tape or paper strips. Ruler.

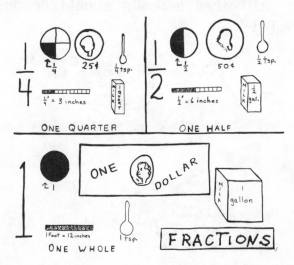

B. Directions for Assembly: On the left side of each section attach the fractions ¼, ½ and the number 1 with plastic tape or paper strips. Add the circles, the money and the appropriate measuring spoon. Draw a foot ruler in each section and color in the area that applies. Attach the milk cartons. Label everything with the felt pen including the section titles. Print the title letters in the lower right corner of the 1 section with the felt pen and outline it with a ruler.

14. THE PUZZLE OF FRACTIONS
(Grades 3-8)

A. Preparation and Materials: Staple a background of your choice to the board. Select a jigsaw you no longer need. If the puzzle is light in color, print the title directly on the puzzle with felt pen. If the puzzle is dark, glue pieces of white paper to the puzzle and print the title on them. All other lettering should be done on white paper circles.

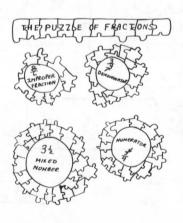

B. Directions for Assembly: Assemble a straight edge of the puzzle and glue to the top of the board for the title. Print the title directly on these puzzle pieces or on a piece of paper glued to these pieces. Assemble several separate puzzle sections. Glue these to the board. On each section glue a circle of paper on which is printed an example of fraction terminology, such as; improper fraction, numerator, denominator, mixed number, etc.

15. EQUIVALENTS (Grades 5-8)

A. Preparation and Materials: Staple a background of your choice to the board. Cut the title letters in a style and from a material of your choice or print them directly on the board with felt pen. On a large sheet of paper draw four concentric circles and divide them into eight equal parts. In each section of the smallest circle write decimal numbers with felt pen.

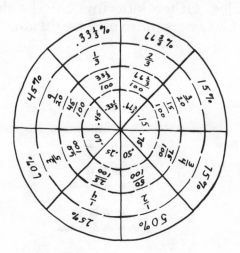

EQUIVALENTS

Working outward write the fractional equivalent, common fraction and percent in each section that refers back to the decimal.

B. Directions for Assembly: Staple the title letters or print them directly across the bottom of the board. Staple the sheet with the circles above the lettering.

C. Variation: Cut four concentric circles, each of a different color. Fasten the centers with a brad. Divide into the eight sections and write the numbers in them. Then move the circles so the numbers are no longer lined up correctly. Have the children straighten them so the decimal to the percent sections all agree.

16. RATIO (Grades 3-8)

A. Preparation and Materials: Staple a background of your choice to the board. Cut the title letters in a style and from a material of your choice. Other lettering can be done with felt pen. Cut one square and two triangles of one

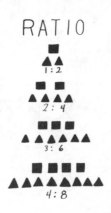

color for the ratio 1:2. Continue with the other ratios making each complete set a different color.

B. Directions for Assembly: Staple title letters to the board. In a pyramid staple the ratios to the board, smallest on top to the largest on the bottom.

17. MONEY (Grades K-3)

A. Preparation and Materials: Staple a solid color-paper or cloth-background to the board. Cut the letters MONEY from aluminum foil in block style. Obtain five small cardboard boxes (jewelry type). Put cotton in the bottom of each one. Make aluminum foil rubbings of a nickel, dime, quarter and half dollar. Use gold foil for the penny. Trim around the edges to

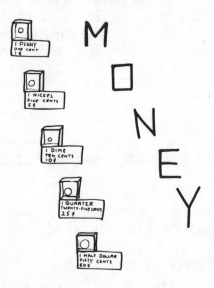

make them round. On pieces of white paper framed with foil write the following labels, one on each piece:

1 Penny one cent 1¢	1 Nickel Five cents 5¢	1 Dime Ten Cents 10¢

1 Quarter Twenty-Five Cents 25¢	1 Half - dollar Fifty cents 50¢

Plastic wrap, tape, glue and pins are also needed.

B. Directions for Assembly: Staple the letters MONEY diagonally on the right side of the board. On the left side pin the boxes diagonally in this order — penny, nickel, dime, quarter and half dollar — leaving room between them for the framed paper labels. Glue the foil coins carefully in the boxes and tape clear plastic wrap tautly over the tops to keep the foil imprints clear. Staple the labels under the boxes.

1 Penny

1 Nickel

Five Pennies = 1 Nickel

Two Nickels = 1 Dime

C. Variation: To show comparative value, use a number of different sixed boxes.

18. BANKING (Grades 5-8)

A. Preparation and Materials: Staple a background of your choice to the board. Cut block style letters to spell the title from play paper money. Gather various sample bank slips (deposit, withdrawal, checks, etc.,) from a local bank or banks, if you have more than one in your community. Fill in the slips with fictitious information. Felt pen.

B. Directions for Assembly: Staple the title letters across the top of the board. Staple the banking slips to the board and label them directly on the board with felt pen.

19. CALENDAR TIME (Grades 2-8)

A. Preparation and Materials: Staple a background of your choice to the board. Obtain three single month sheets from a fairly large

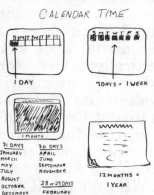

calendar. You may want to choose examples of 28, 30 and 31 day months. Obtain a complete year calendar that is also fairly large. Cut enough squares of colored paper, to be glued on the single month sheets, to block out a day, a week and a whole month. Felt pen.

B. Directions for Assembly: Print the title across the top of the board with felt pen. Staple the three single calendar months to the board. Glue on the colored squares blocking out a day on one, a week on another and the whole month on the third. With felt pen draw arrows to the squares on each sheet and label what they illustrate. Staple the full calendar to the board and label. In the remaining board room label and list the months with 28, 30 and 31 days.

20. TELLING TIME (Grades 2-8)

A. Preparation and Materials: Staple a background of fabric, foil or paper in any color to the board. Cut three large rectangles from tagboard or other heavy paper using light colors if possible. At the top of one rectangle print the words WE BEGIN SCHOOL AT 9:00 with felt pen. Draw three round clock faces and one digital clock shape vertically. Use three different numbering systems on the round

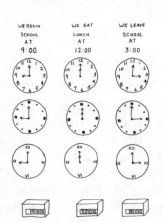

faces with hands pointing to 9:00. On the digital clock write 900. Be sure to write the times on these clocks that apply to your particular school. (These times are only examples.) At the top of the second rectangle print WE EAT LUNCH AT 12:00. Follow the same procedure as the first rectangle changing time to 12:00. At the top of the third rectangle print WE LEAVE SCHOOL AT 3:00 and add the clocks reading 3:00.

B. Directions for Assembly: Staple the rectangles to the board. If there is any room remaining, print the title letters across the top of the board.

C. Variations: 1. Put rectangles on the board and add a different clock each day.

2. Use brads to make hands on the clocks movable and use a variety of headings to tell what time various activities begin, e.g., TODAY WE HAVE RECESS AT 10:15 or TODAY WE HAVE MUSIC AT 2:00.

21. MEASUREMENT (Grades 2-8)

A. Preparation and Materials: Staple a background of your choice to the board. Cut out a one inch square piece of colored paper. Cut four separate strips of colored paper, one inch high and twelve inches long. Mark off the inches with felt pen. Draw a silly foot, twelve inches long directly on the board, centered near the top. Draw three more silly feet, each twelve inches long and next to each other to form a yard, diagonally in the center of the board. Draw one more silly foot larger than the others at the bottom of the board. Print the title on this foot.

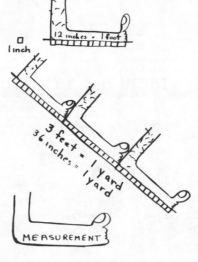

B. Directions for Assembly: Staple the one inch square to the top, left of the single silly foot. Label it ONE INCH with felt pen. Print 12 INCHES = 1 FOOT on the single foot and staple a foot long strip beneath it. Staple the three other foot long strips under the three diagonal feet. Label 3 FEET = 1 YARD, 36 INCHES = 1 YARD.

22. THE METRIC SYSTEM (Grades 3-8)

A. Preparation and Materials: Staple a background of your choice to the board. Cut block style letters to spell THE METRIC SYSTEM, VOLUME and WEIGHT in a color compatible with your background choice. For the top half of the board you will need a one ounce plastic cup (cold medicine or cough syrup dispenser), a clean one quart milk carton, the

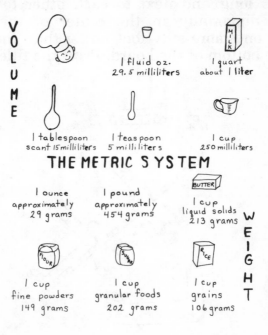

VOLUME

1 fluid oz.
29.5 milliliters

1 quart
about 1 liter

1 tablespoon
scant 15 milliliters

1 teaspoon
5 milliliters

1 cup
250 milliliters

THE METRIC SYSTEM

1 ounce
approximately
29 grams

1 pound
approximately
454 grams

BUTTER
1 cup
liquid solids
213 grams

1 cup
fine powders
149 grams

1 cup
granular foods
202 grams

1 cup
grains
106 grams

WEIGHT

tablespoon and teaspoon from a set of measuring spoons and a plastic measuring cup. For the bottom section you will need an empty pound butter (or margarine) box, an empty flour bag (two pound, if possible), an empty sugar bag and an empty rice box. Felt pen.

B. Directions for Assembly: Staple the words THE METRIC SYSTEM across the center of the board, the word VOLUME vertically at the upper left and the word WEIGHT vertically at the bottom right. Draw the chef's head at the top right on the board. In line with it, attach the one ounce cup labeling it 1 FLUID OZ., 29.5 MILLILITERS and the quart milk carton labeling it 1 QUART, ABOUT 1 LITER with the felt pen. In the next line attach the tablespoon labeling it 1 TABLESPOON, SCANT 15 MILLILITERS; the teaspoon labeling it 1 TEASPOON, 5 MILLILITERS and the measuring cup labeling it 1 CUP, 250 MILLILITERS. To assemble the first line of the bottom section, print 1 OUNCE APPROXIMATELY 29 GRAMS and 1 POUND, APPROXIMATELY 454 GRAMS and attach the butter box labeling it 1 CUP LIQUID SOLIDS, 213 GRAMS. In the second line attach the flour bag labeling it 1 CUP FINE POWDERS, 149 GRAMS; the sugar bag labeling it 1 CUP GRANULATED FOODS, 202 GRAMS and the rice box labeling it 1 CUP GRAINS, 106 GRAMS.

23. GEOMETRIC FIGURES (Grades 4-8)

A. Preparation and Materials: Staple any bright colored background to the board. Using yarn and heavy starch, dip and shape the title letters and geometric shapes. Lay them on a flat surface to dry. Felt pen.

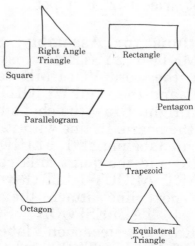

GEOMETRIC FIGURES

Square

Right Angle Triangle

Rectangle

Parallelogram

Pentagon

Octagon

Trapezoid

Equilateral Triangle

B. Directions for Assembly: Staple the title and figures to the board. Print the names directly on the board under the figures with the felt pen.

C. Variation: Make boards representing specific types of geometric figures, e.g., three sided figures, such as triangles.

24. P = PERIMETER (Grades 5-8)

A. Preparation and Materials: Staple a background of your choice in a light color to the board. Cut title letters in a style and from a material of your choice or print them directly on the board. Cut the geometric shapes from colored paper or colored tagboard. Felt pen.

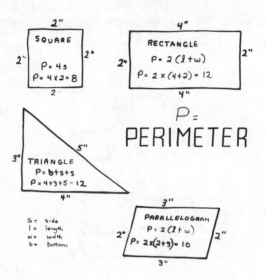

B. Directions for Assembly: Staple the title or letter it directly on the board. Staple the shapes to the board and write the names and formulas for the figures directly on them with felt pen. Write the inch dimensions on the outside edges of each shape. In the lower left segment of the board write the key to the initials used in the perimeter formulas.

25. A = AREA (Grades 5-8)

A. Preparation and Materials: Staple a white wrapping paper or shelf paper background to the board. Next use a sheet of paper that is the same size as the board or tape several sheets together. This can be gift wrap or shelf paper, but it should have a pattern or be colored. Draw a = AREA at the top of this paper in block style letters. Using small, sharp scissors, cut out the letters carefully. Be careful not to tear the large sheet. Discard cutout letters. Draw on various geometric figures, cut them out and discard. Felt pen.

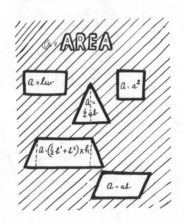

B. Directions for Assembly: Staple the cutout sheet to the board over the white background. Outline the letters and shapes with felt pen. Inside each figure on the white paper write the formulas for the figures.

26. AREA OF A CIRCLE (Grades 4-8)

A. Preparation and Materials: Staple a background of your choice to the board. Cut the title letters in block style from colored paper compatible with the background. Cut a large circle almost the same size as the board from the same colored paper as the title letters. Divide the circle into three equal sections horizontally with plastic tape, paper strips, or felt pen. For the top section cut out a picture of a pie from a magazine, a block style R and a square from colored paper. For both the center and bottom sections cut one colored paper circle. Felt pen.

AREA OF A CIRCLE

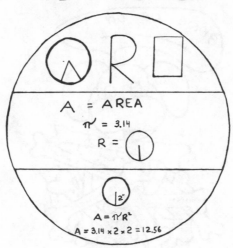

B. Directions for Assembly: Staple the title letters across the top of the board. Center the large circle in the remaining board room and staple it. Letter the center section with felt pen. Staple the small circle after the R = and draw in the radius. Staple the other small circle in the bottom section, draw on the radius and label it 2 inches. Write in the other information.

27. BONE UP ON _____ (Grades 2-8)

A. Preparation and Materials: Staple a yellow background to the board. Cut the thought bubble for the title from white paper. Cut the head, underjaw, ears and two paws for the puppy from dark brown paper. Cut the jowls from light brown paper, the tongue from red, the eyes from white, pupils from dark brown and nose circle from black. Draw a pile of bones on white paper and cut around the edges. Felt pen and glue.

B. Directions for Assembly: Print the title inside the thought bubble and staple it to the board. Staple the head, ear, jaws and jowls of the puppy to the board. Glue on the eyes, pupils, nose and tongue. Print mathematical terms on some of the bones and staple the paper bones under the puppy's head. Glue the paws onto the top bone. Fill in the blank in the title with the appropriate subject.

C. Variation: Make several title bubbles and bone sets. Fill in the blank in the title with a different subject and make the bone sets apply with corresponding vocabulary, e.g., social studies (title), Latitude, Longitude, Prime Meridian, etc. (bones).

28. SNOW JOB (Grades 4-8)

A. Preparation and Materials: Staple a blue background to the board. Cut blue block style letters to spell the title. Cut any number of circles from fairly heavy white paper to represent snowflakes. Write brain teasers on strips of paper and glue onto the snowflake circles. Cotton batting, cotton balls and glue are also needed. Pins are optional.

SNOW JOB

B. Directions for Assembly: Glue cotton batting to the bottom six or eight inches of the board (depends on the size of the board). Glue title letters onto this cotton border. Staple the snowflakes to the board and glue borders of cotton balls onto them. If you pin the snowflakes to the board, you can change them more easily.

SECTION V: "SCIENCE"

This section will help you set up bulletin boards about biology, zoology, nutrition, personal care, physical sciences and ecology.

1. THE ANIMAL KINGDOM (Grades 3-8)

A. Preparation and Materials: Staple a black background to the board. Cut a large

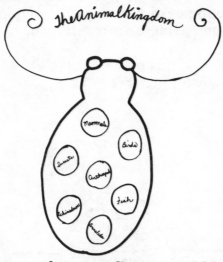

ladybug from red paper. Cut several black paper circles. Write the divisions of the animal kingdom on these with gold ink. Gold braid, glue and two gold buttons or yellow gumdrops are also needed.

B. Directions for Assembly: Staple the ladybug to the board and glue on the black circles. Staple some of the gold braid to the board to form antennae. Glue the buttons or gumdrops to the head of the bug for eyes. Staple more gold braid to the board to spell the title.

2. BE INFORMED ABOUT BIOLOGICAL SCIENCES (Grades 4-8)

A. Preparation and Materials: Staple a blue background to the top three-fourths of the board for sky and green to the bottom one-fourth for grass. Cut block style letters from yellow paper to spell the title starting with the word INFORMED. Cut a large beehive from the same yellow paper as well as several bee bodies. Cut the wings from rice paper, napkins, foil or tissue paper. Glue and a felt pen.

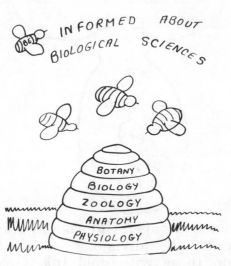

B. Directions for Assembly: Staple the beehive to the board centered in the grassy area. Use the felt pen to draw in the section lines and letter the sciences. Glue the wings to the bees and staple them to the board. Fill in detail lines and stingers with felt pen. Staple one bee in the upper left corner and write BE on it for the first word in the title. Staple the rest of the title letters to the board.

3. UNDERSEA WORLD (Grades 3-8)

A. Preparation and Materials: Staple a blue background to the board. Draw or cut out pictures of whimsical undersea creatures. Cut a gray paper round porthole frame to enclose the creature pictures. Cut free form letters from dark blue paper. Clear cellophane or plastic wrap.

B. Directions for Assembly: Staple the creature pictures to the board and cover them with the cellophane or plastic wrap. Staple the porthole frame to enclose the picture. Trim away any excess cellophane or plastic wrap. Staple the title letters under the picture.

4. CLASSIFICATION OF PLANTS
(Grades 5-8)

A. Preparation and Materials: Staple a brown paper background to the board. Divide the board into four equal sections vertically. Cut yellow paper strips to mark the divisions. For the first section cut small block style letters to spell THALLOPHYTA and free form shapes from yellow paper. Draw simple sketches of plants in this phylum on white paper that will fit on the free form shapes. Color them if you wish and label them with felt pen. For the second section cut light blue block style letters

—119—

to spell BRYOPHYTA and free form shapes. Draw plants in this phylum on pieces of white paper. Color them if you choose and label them with felt pen. For the third section cut the letters to spell PTERIDOPHYTA and free form shapes from light green. Draw the plants in this phylum on white paper and label them. Color if you choose. Cut a pink paper strip to divide the fourth section in half horizontally. Cut the letters to spell SPERMATOPHYTA and free form shapes from pink paper. Draw plants in this phylum on white paper and label them. Color if you choose. Cut block style letters to spell the title from light green paper. Glue and felt pen.

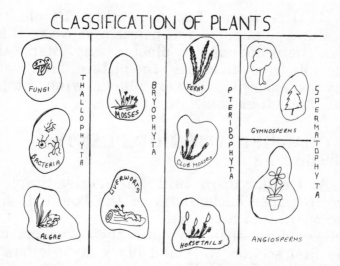

B. Directions for Assembly: Staple the title letters across the top of the board. Outline four board sections with the yellow paper strips. Divide the fourth section in half with the pink paper strip. Staple the THALLOPHYTA letters in the first section vertically. Glue the drawings onto the yellow free form shapes and staple to the board. Staple the BRYOPHYTA letters in the second section. Glue the pictures onto the blue free form shapes and staple onto the board. Staple the PTERIDOPHYTA letters in the third section. Glue the pictures onto the light green free form shapes and staple to the board. Staple the SPERMATOPHYTA letters in the fourth section. Label the top section GYMNOSPERMS with felt pen. Label the bottom section ANGIOSPERMS directly on the board with felt pen. Glue the picture onto the pink shape and staple to the board.

5. TREE TALK (Grades 5-8)

A. Preparation and Materials: Staple a light blue background to the top two-thirds of the board for the sky and a black or brown background to the bottom one-third of the board for the ground. Collect a real twig to fit the size of your board and several real fall colored leaves. To preserve these leaves, press them with a warm iron between sheets of waxed paper. Use a towel over the top sheet of waxed paper so the wax doesn't stick to your iron. When cool, peel the waxed paper from the leaves. Cut small pieces of paper, white or colored and write tree

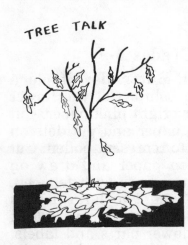

terms on them, such as; PHOTOSYNTHESIS, CHLOROPHYLL, TERMINAL BUD, etc. Glue and pins. Cut black or brown free form letters to spell the title.

B. Directions for Assembly: Staple the title letters at the top of the board. Pin the twig to the board to represent a tree. Pin, staple or glue the leaves to the board so they look like they are falling from the "tree." Glue the pieces of paper with the terms on them to these leaves. Attach extra leaves around the base of the "tree."

C. Variation: Make the bulletin board pertain to one specific aspect of tree identification. For example, use a number of smaller twigs with each showing one specific type of leaf veining, shape, etc.

6. FLOWER PARTS (Grades 5-8)

A. Preparation and Materials: Staple a white background to the board. Cut the flower petals from yellow, red or bright pink paper. Cut four stamens from white paper and put dots on the anthers with felt pen to represent pollen. Cut the pistil from light green paper and draw on the ovaries, eggs and detail lines with felt pen. Cut two sepals, a stem and two large leaves from darker green paper. Cut narrow black paper strips to connect flower parts and labels. Cut paper for labels from the same color as the flower part, i.e., yellow, red, or bright pink for the petal label, etc. Label according to the illustration. Print PARTS OF A FLOWER on a piece of tagboard for the title. Glue.

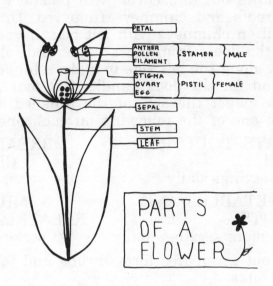

B. Directions for Assembly: Staple the flower petals, sepals, stem and leaves to the board. First glue the stamens onto the petals and then glue the pistil in the center of the flower base. Staple the black strips leading from each separate flower part. Add the labels. Staple the title in the lower right portion of the board.

7. OPEN THE DOORS TO GOOD NUTRITION (Grades 3-6)

A. Preparation and Materials: Staple a blue background to the top two-thirds of the board for sky and green to the bottom one-third for grass. Cut out three free form white clouds to print the title on, two words on each cloud. Cut four white rectangles for the houses adding wood and window detail with felt pen or cut windows out and cover with plastic wrap. Cut the roofs and chimneys from red. Draw brick detail on chimneys with felt pen, if you choose. Cut the doors from black paper and fold a strip back along the left side to make a hinge. Attach a brad for the door handle. Cut four pieces of white paper the size of the finished door and write one of the following on each one:

MEATS, POULTRY, FISH
1-2 servings daily

BREADS AND CEREALS
3-4 servings daily

VEGETABLES AND FRUITS
4 or more servings daily

MILK AND RELATED FOODS
2-3 servings daily

Cut out green free form shrubs and four white sidewalks.

B. Directions for Assembly: Staple the four houses to the board. Add the roofs and chimneys. Glue one white paper with the food groups to each doorway. Cut a slit on the right side of this paper and through the house so the brad can act as a door latch. Glue on the doors, shrubs and sidewalks. Print the title letters on the clouds and staple above the houses.

8. GOOD HEALTH (Grades 3-8)

A. Preparation and Materials: Staple a background of your choice to the board. Mark divisions lightly on the board with a pencil. Cut out the children's heads and draw on the features with felt pen. Glue on yarn for the boy's hair. For the girl make yarn pigtails, tie the ends with bows and glue onto the head. Cut colored paper circles for the center sections of the board (optional). More yarn, starch and/or glue.

B. Directions for Assembly: Glue yarn over pencil lines to make board divisions. Form title letters with yarn by gluing them directly onto the board or by dipping them in heavy starch, forming the letters and laying them on a flat surface to dry. Then staple them to the board and attach the children's heads. For the three center sections either glue the words directly onto the board, onto the colored paper circles, or starch and staple them to the board.

9. GOOD GROOMING (Grades 3-8)

A. Preparation and Materials: Staple a dark colored paper background to the board. Cut a large free form shape from a lighter colored paper and staple to the board. Cut the title letters from the darker background color in block style. For the other lettering cut free form letters, magazine letters, or label with felt pen. Obtain a comb and shampoo box, toothbrush and toothpaste box, washcloth and bar soap wrapper, shoe polish box and a detergent box and an article of doll clothing. Glue and felt pen.

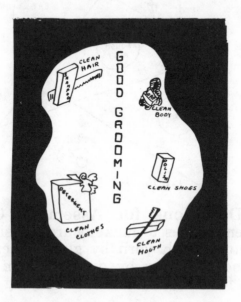

B. Directions for Assembly: Staple the title letters vertically in the center of the free form shape. Glue the comb to the board and staple the shampoo box over it. Label this CLEAN HAIR. Glue the toothbrush to the board and staple the toothpaste box over it. Label these items CLEAN MOUTH. Staple the washcloth and soap wrapper to the board and label CLEAN BODY. Staple the shoe polish box to the board and label CLEAN SHOES. Staple the detergent box to the board and have the article of doll clothing stuck in the top of the box. Label this CLEAN CLOTHES.

10. BRUSH YOUR TEETH OFTEN (Grades 2-8)

A. Preparation and Materials: Staple a background of your choice to the board. Use magazine cutouts or cut free form letters to spell the title from material compatible with the background. Obtain an almost empty toothpaste tube, a toothbrush, white yarn or gift tie and glue.

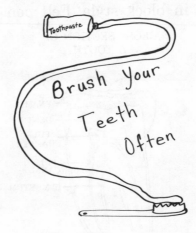

B. Directions for Assembly: Be sure the toothpaste is well back in the tube and seal the end with glue. Attach the tube to the top of the board and the toothbrush to the bottom. Glue the white yarn from the tube to the brush to represent toothpaste. Staple the title letters to the board.

C. Variation: Staple many tubes or boxes of dentifrice cleaners in scatter formation on the board. Also, randomly attach toothbrushes and dental floss containers to the board. Leave space for lettering.

11. CROSS SECTION OF A TOOTH (Grades 4-8)

A. Preparation and Materials: Staple a red background to the board. Cut block style title letters. Cut the tooth sections from different colors of paper; enamel-white, dentin-yellow, pulp-red. Cut them all the same shape except reduce the size of the dentin and pulp as you cut. Cut strips of black paper to go from tooth parts to labels. Cut label letters from black or white paper in block style. Felt pen and pins.

CROSS SECTION OF
A TOOTH

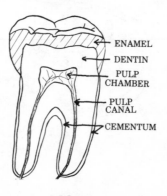

ENAMEL

DENTIN

PULP
CHAMBER

PULP
CANAL

CEMENTUM

B. Directions for Assembly: Staple the title letters to the top of the board. Staple the white enamel to the board, add the dentin over it and then the pulp. Staple the strips and labels to the board or write this with felt pen.

12. BLOOD (Grades 4-8)

A. Preparation and Materials: Staple a light blue or a black background to the board. Cut out large block style red letters to spell BLOOD. Cut three blood drops to drip from the title letters. Cut a circle from red tagboard to represent a red cell. Use a felt pen to draw on the face. Attach pipe cleaners to the back side of the circle for arms and legs. Bend them as they appear in the illustration. Cut a piece of white tagboard for the sign the cell is carrying and print RED CELLS CARRY OXYGEN on it. Cut a circle from white tagboard for a white cell. Draw on the face and attach the pipe cleaner arms and legs. Cut a sign from tagboard for this cell to carry and print WHITE CELLS FIGHT INFECTION on it. Cut a plasma bottle from yellow tagboard. Draw on the face, attach the pipe cleaners and make a sign to read PLASMA IS THE LIQUID PART OF BLOOD.

B. Directions for Assembly: Staple the title letters and blood drops vertically to the left side of the board. Staple the red blood cell and sign to the upper left part of the board, the white cell and sign to the center right and the plasma bottle and sign to the lower left.

13. ADD-A-BONE (Grades 6-8)

A. Preparation and Materials: Staple a black paper background to the board. Buy a Halloween skeleton (several if they are small and difficult to cut apart) and cut apart the individual bones. Print the names of the bones on pieces of white paper. Cut a large bone shape from white paper and print the title on it with felt pen. Pins.

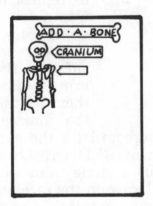

B. Directions for Assembly: Staple the title bone to the top of the board. Hand each child either a bone or a piece of paper with the name of the bone on it and a pin. Starting with the skull, have the child with that bone staple it to the board. Then have the child with the label pin it to the board. Continue until the skeleton is complete.

C. Variation: Have the children make bones from tagboard to scale.

14. FLUOROSCOPE (Grades 4-8)

A. Preparation and Materials: Staple a background of your choice to the board. Draw a picture of a person directly on the board or use a large paper doll. Cut a piece of tagboard to fit between the shoulders and hips of your drawing or the paper doll. Sketch organs of the body on this and label them with felt pen. Cover with plastic wrap and attach a black paper or tape border around the edges. Cut white block style letters to spell the title.

FLUOROSCOPE

B. Directions for Assembly: Staple the paper doll person to the board if that is what you are using. Attach the tagboard between the shoulders and the hips. Staple the title letters across the top of the board and outline them with felt pen.

15. PUZZLE OF THE MIND (Grades 6-8)

A. Preparation and Materials: Staple a background of your choice to the board. Cut

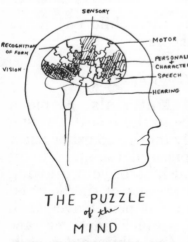

letters to spell the title in a style and from materials you choose. Cut the profile of a head and the outline of a brain with brain stem that will fit inside the profile. Draw jigsaw puzzle lines on the brain and color various pieces different colors to represent brain areas. Felt pen and glue.

B. Directions for Assembly: Staple the profile to the board. Glue the brain and brain stem inside the head. Using the felt pen, draw lines leading from the various colored areas and label the brain functions outside the head profile. Staple the title letters at the bottom of the board.

16. THE PHYSICAL SCIENCES (Grades 4-8)

A. Preparation and Materials: This background is put on by sections so that you may remove each section intact and use it as a basis for another board. Cut black block style lettering for all sections or print directly on the paper with felt pen. Cut pieces of heavy white paper to fit board sections as shown in the illustration. Cut black paper strips to cover the lines between the sections. Cut out small pictures of levers, rocks, mountains and a weather map from magazines or newspapers. From

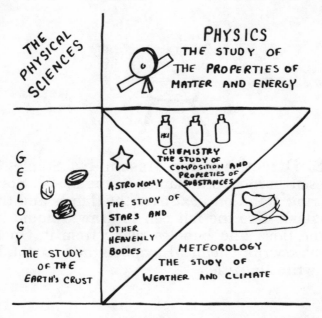

The Physical Sciences

PHYSICS
THE STUDY OF THE PROPERTIES OF MATTER AND ENERGY

GEOLOGY
THE STUDY OF THE EARTH'S CRUST

ASTRONOMY
THE STUDY OF STARS AND OTHER HEAVENLY BODIES

CHEMISTRY
THE STUDY OF COMPOSITION AND PROPERTIES OF SUBSTANCES

METEOROLOGY
THE STUDY OF WEATHER AND CLIMATE

white paper cut out three chemical bottles, outline with felt pen and write a chemical formula on each one (HCL, H_2O, H_2SO_4, NaCL, etc.). Either cut out a large gold star or obtain one already made. If for some reason you cannot find these items, draw them directly on the board in the appropriate section. Glue and pins.

17. CHEMICAL ELEMENTS (Grades 5-8)

A. Preparation and Materials: Staple a background of your choice directly on the board. Form the flask with florist wire and cover with plastic tape. Cut the ring stand and Bunsen burner from black paper. Cut the burner flames from light blue and cream colored paper. Crinkle to resemble flames. Felt pen.

B. Directions for Assembly: Staple the Bunsen burner and flames to the board. Staple the ring stand on next over the flames and then the flask. Use the felt pen to draw a liquid line in the flask and bubbles rising from it. On the bubbles write chemical symbols and in the liquid write the title.

18. HEAT (Grades 4-8)

A. Preparation and Materials: Staple a background of your choice to the board. Either

cut the necessary top lettering in a style and from materials of your choice or print directly on the board with felt pen. Cut black paper strips to divide the board as shown in the illustration. For the left side cut a sun and its rays from yellow paper. Make the iron from aluminum foil or cut a

—134—

picture from a magazine. Draw a window or outline one with plastic tape. Cut a picture of a radiator from a magazine. For the right side, cut ovals of paper and print scrambled vocabulary words dealing with heat on them.

B. Directions for Assembly: Staple or print the top lettering onto the board. Staple on the division strips. Add the pictures and their labels to the left side and the scrambled word ovals on the right.

19. THERMOMETERS (Grades 4-8)

A. Preparation and Materials: Staple a background of your choice to the board. Cut four heavy white paper rectangles to be used for thermometer mountings. Use four clear plastic straws or plastic tubing for the thermometers. Cut four thin red strips to be placed behind the tubes to show degree levels. Glue and felt pen.

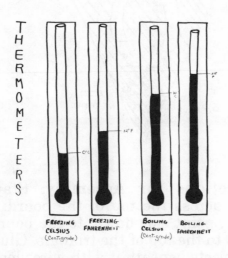

THERMOMETERS

FREEZING CELSIUS (Centigrade) FREEZING FAHRENHEIT BOILING CELSIUS (Centigrade) BOILING FAHRENHEIT

B. Directions for Assembly: Staple the thermometer mountings to the board. Glue the red degree level strips onto the mountings and glue the tubes over them. With felt pen write the title vertically along the left side of the board and add labels under the appropriate thermometers. Write the degrees alongside the top of the degree levels.

20. MAGNETS (Grades 3-8)

A. Preparation and Materials: Staple an aluminum foil background to the board. Cut black block style letters to spell the title. From black tagboard cut a large triangle. Obtain a small horseshoe shaped magnet, metal wire and other metal objects, glue and a felt pen.

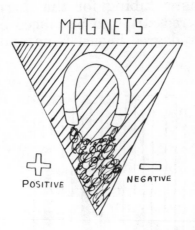

B. Directions for Assembly: Staple the title letters across the top of the board. Attach the triangle, point side down, to the board. Glue the magnet to the top of the triangle. Glue metal wire and objects beneath it with wires leading to the ends of the magnet. On the sides of the triangle point draw a plus sign and label it POSITIVE and a negative sign and label it NEGATIVE.

21. ROCKS (Grades 5-8)

A. Preparation and Materials: Staple a background of your choice to the board. Either cut the lettering in a style and from a material of your choice or print directly on the board. Divide the board into sections as shown in the illustration. Cut three pieces of paper and write examples of igneous rocks on one, sedimentary rocks on another and meta- morphic rocks on the third. Cut out a picture of a volcano or draw one. Cut red or orange cellophane for flames. Cut a piece of sandpaper for the base of the sedimentary section and a piece of blue paper crumpled to resemble water to go over the sand- paper. Felt pen and black plastic tape.

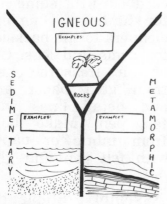

B. Directions for Assembly: Cover the dividing lines between the sections with plastic tape. Add the lettering to the sections as well as the papers with the examples of rocks. Staple the volcano and flames just above the title triangle in the Igneous section. Staple the sand- paper and blue paper water at the bottom of the Sedimentary section, and draw a picture of the layers of the earth at the bottom of the Metamorphic section.

22. TREASURES OF THE EARTH
(Grades 4-8)

A. Preparation and Materials: Staple a dark blue background to the board. Cut dark

blue block style letters to spell the title. Cut out a picture of a globe and glue it to a piece of cardboard the same size for sturdiness. Glue pipe cleaners to the backside for arms and legs. Cut out a treasure chest from gold paper and add detail lines with felt pen. Make bags from fabric or paper. Print labels on them with felt pen and glue to the chest.

B. Directions for Assembly: Staple the globe to the board and the chest above it. Position the pipe cleaner arms and legs. The arms should appear to be holding up the chest.

23. WEATHER MAP (Grades 4-8)

A. Preparation and Materials: Staple a background of your choice to the board. Cut black block style letters to spell the title. Obtain a large map of the United States, some grease pencils and a sheet of heavy plastic large enough to cover the entire board.

B. Directions for Assembly: Staple the title letters to the top of the board and the map beneath them. Cover the entire board with the plastic. Have the children write the daily weather symbols on the board with the grease pencils. They can get the weather from the newspaper, T.V., or by calling the weather bureau.

WEATHER MAP

24. PRECIPITATION (Grades 5-8)

A. Preparation and Materials: Staple a black background to the board. Cut light gray block style letters to spell the title and section labels. Divide the board into sections as shown in the illustration. Cut paper strips or use plastic tape to cover the pencil lines. Cut four gray clouds, one for each section. Tear off a piece of plastic wrap and shred part way up to resemble rain. Use clear straws or pipe cleaners with glitter glued to them for sleet. Cover cotton balls with plastic wrap for hail. Cut small paper snowflakes or use cotton balls for snow.

B. Directions for Assembly: Staple the title letters to the top of the board and the other labels at the base of each section. Cover the division lines with paper strips or tape. In the top left section staple the plastic wrap first and then the cloud over it. In the top right section staple or glue the materials simulating sleet; then staple the cloud to the board. In the lower left section staple the cloud first and then glue the covered cotton balls in scatter formation. In the lower right section, staple the cloud and glue on the snowflakes or cotton balls.

25. SPEED OF LIGHT (Grades 6-8)

A. Preparation and Materials: Staple a background of your choice to the board. Cut a

large turtle, head, shell, tail and four legs from dark green paper. Cut lighter green block style letters for the title and spots to fit on the shell.

Print a statement about the speed of light on each spot. The following are examples:

1. Light travels around the earth seven times in one second.
2. The distance of the Sun from Earth is 93,000,000 miles.
3. The speed of light is 186,000 miles per second.
4. The number of seconds for the Sun's light to reach Earth is 93,000,000 ÷ 186,000 = 500 seconds.
5. Light travels around the earth 60 × 7 = 420 times in one minute.
6. The speed of light in one-half minute: 30 × 186,000 = 5,580,000 miles.

Glue.

B. Directions for Assembly: Staple the title letters to the top of the board. Staple the turtles shell to the center of the board and glue on the remaining turtle parts. Glue the spots onto the shell.

26. BEYOND THE EARTH (Grades 5-8)

A. Preparation and Materials: Staple a background of your choice to the board. Cut a circle segment to fit across the bottom of the board to represent the earth. Make the spaceship from colored paper. Use yarn or cotton for the exhaust. Felt pen, glue.

B. Directions for Assembly: Staple the segment of earth to the bottom of the board. Letter the title on the spaceship with felt pen and staple to the board. Glue the exhaust at the base. Add curved lines above the earth to indicate the regions of the atmosphere and label them.

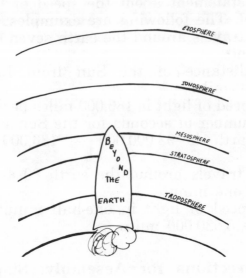

27. THE UNIVERSE (Grades 3-8)

A. Preparation and Materials: Staple a black background to the board. Cut out a large gold star and print on it the title letters. Cut four slightly curved strips of white paper to fit from the star to the edge of the board. Print spatial information on these. The following statements could be used:

1. PLANETS: Saturn is the planet with three rings around it.

2. STARS: The North Star is the last star in the handle of the Little Dipper.

3. COMETS: Halley's Comet returns approximately every 76 years, due again in 1986.

4. METEOR SHOWERS: Meteor showers are due many times during the year.

Cut additional strips for other space facts. Pins.

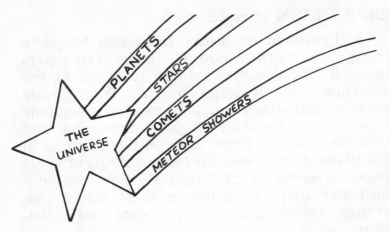

PLANETS

STARS

COMETS

METEOR SHOWERS

THE UNIVERSE

B. Directions for Assembly: Staple the star in the lower left area of the board. Pin the curved strips from the star to the edge of the board. Change them often to continue interest in the board.

28. LOOK UP (Grades 3-8)

A. Preparation and Materials: Staple a black background to the board, solid or in separate sheets. Cut white block style letters to spell the title. Use small gummed stars to form various constellations, with the different colors representing key stars and varying degrees of heat. If you put these stars on separate sheets of black paper, you can use them again. Cut slips of white paper and print the constellation names on them. Pins (optional).

B. Directions for Assembly: Glue the stars to the board in the constellation shapes or on separate sheets of black paper. Attach the name labels. If you use separate sheets, pin them to the board so they can be more easily removed for use again.

29. A PRISM (Grades 5-8)

A. Preparation and Materials: Staple a background to the board. Cut block style letters to spell the title from different colors of the spectrum. Cut a large triangle from heavy plastic and attach small pieces of cellophane tape to the backside to give dimension and indicate a prism. Draw lines on the prism as in the illustration. Cut eight narrow strips of white paper to represent eight rays. Cut seven slightly narrower strips of paper in these colors: red, orange, yellow, green, blue, indigo and violet. Glue.

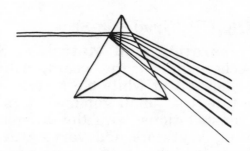

B. Directions for Assembly: Staple the title letters to the top of the board. Glue the triangle to the center of the board. Next glue the eight white strips, one leading to the prism from the left edge and the remaining seven as rays broken by the prism. Glue the colored strips onto these white ones in the following order from the top: red, orange, yellow, green, indigo and violet.

30. ECOLOGY (Grades 4-8)

A. Preparation and Materials: Staple a blue (sky) background to the top two-thirds of the board and a green (ground) background to the bottom one-third. Cut bright green block style letters to spell the title, yellow block letters to spell GOOD SENSE SAVES and dark gray block letters to spell POLLUTION KILLS. Divide the board into sections as shown in the illustration. Cut paper strips to cover division lines or use tape. From the Good Sense side, cut blue paper to represent clean water and cover with plastic wrap or cellophane. Cut out a yellow sun and add a happy face with felt pen. Cut some fish and add happy faces and detail lines. Cut the tree trunk from dark brown paper; the foliage from green; the flowers from any bright colors; their center from yellow, brown, or green; and the stems and leaves from green. For the Pollution side cut a yellow sun but add a sad

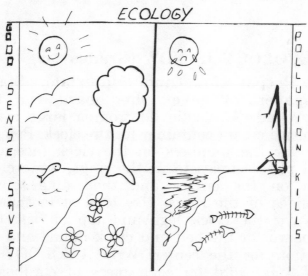

face and tears. Instead of a tree, cut some broken branches with no foliage. Cut sandpaper to cover part of the green background and small dark blue circles to represent muddy puddles. Gray or some other dull colored cellophane.

B. Directions for Assembly: Staple the title letters to the top of the board, GOOD SENSE SAVES vertically along the left edge and POLLUTION KILLS vertically along the right edge. Cover the division lines on the board with paper strips or tape. Cover part of the green background on the left side with the plastic covered blue paper and add the fish. Draw sea gulls in the sky area and add the flowers and the tree in the land area. On the right side glue the blue circle to the sandpaper and staple over part of the green. Draw on some fish skeletons and add the broken branches. Cover this entire side of the board with the gray or dull colored cellophane.

31. ECOLOGY IS NOW (Grades 4-8)

A. Preparation and Materials: Staple newspaper to cover the board for the background. A plastic lid from a large coffee can or ice cream container for the clock. Pop top rings for the numbers on the clock face. Cut small paper circles to fit the rings, write clock hours on the circles and then glue to the backsides of the rings. Use tops of toothpaste tubes for the clock legs and top of bell. Cut cardboard for the bell and clock hands and use a button for the center. Write ECOLOGY IS NOW, one word on each piece of cardboard.

Strips of paper with ecological ideas written on them (organic gardening, return bottles, recycled paper, conserve fuel, etc.). Pins or staple gun and a felt pen.

B. Directions for Assembly: Attach clock to the board with pins or staple gun. Add the bell and feet in the same manner. Glue on the rings to form the clock face and attach hands. Draw a line from the clock numbers out to the side of the clock and attach a strip of paper with an ecological idea written on it.

32. BRIGHT IDEAS (Grades 3-8)

A. Preparation and Materials: Staple a black background to the board. Cut black block style letters to spell the title. Cut as many light bulbs as you want from white paper. Cut as many small yellow squares as you cut bulbs for the bases. Glue these onto the bulbs and add detail lines with felt pen. Print the name of an inventor and his invention on each light bulb. Cut a large piece of foil to hold the title letters and foil strips to go from the title to the light bulbs.

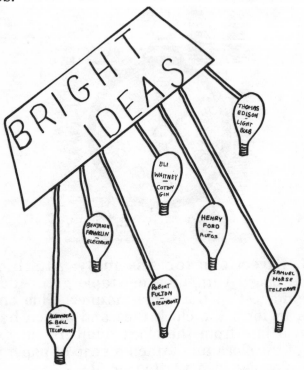

B. Directions for Assembly: Staple the large piece of foil to the upper left corner. Glue on the title letters and the foil strips. Add the light bulbs at the ends of the strips.

C. Variations: 1. Find pictures of inventors and staple to the board. Glue a light bulb over the inventor's head.

2. Cut out one large light bulb and list inventors and their inventions on it.

SECTION VI: "JUST BECAUSE"

This section will show you how to make seasonal, safety and holiday boards. The put-on list will give you more ideas for non-subject areas.

1. FALL (Grades K-8)

A. Preparation and Materials: Staple a black background to the board. Collect and wax fall colored leaves. Cut a large orange pumpkin from shiny gift wrap or construction paper, the stem from tan paper and add detail lines with

felt pen. Collect some corn stalks. Cut and split them so they will fit on your board. Cut black block style letters to spell FALL and to fit on the pumpkin. Glue.

B. Directions for Assembly: Staple the leaves along the bottom and up the right side of the board. Attach the corn stalk in the shape of a shock to the left of the center. Staple the pumpkin in the lower right corner and glue on the title letters.

2. WINTERTIME IS FUNTIME (Grades K-8)

A. Preparation and Materials: Staple a blue background to the board. Cut title letters from tagboard and glue cotton on them to represent snow. Collect a child's knitted cap, muffler and mittens (lightly stuffed). Cut yarn for hair and facial features from colored paper. More cotton, pins and glue.

WINTERTIME
IS
FUN TIME

B. Directions for Assembly: Staple the title letters at the bottom of the board. Pin on the child's cap and attach the yarn hair under it. Staple or glue on the facial features. Tie the muffler as if it were around a child's neck and pin it to the board. Pin the mittens to the board at the wrists and fill the palms with cotton to represent a snowball.

3. SPRING IS HERE! (Grades K-8)

A. Preparation and Materials: Staple a light blue background to the board. Cut free form letters to spell the title. Cut fifteen flower petals from shocking pink paper, fifteen smaller petals from lighter pink paper, three stems in varying lengths and several free form leaves from green paper. Use three styrofoam balls for the flower centers. Cut wide strips of green paper to fit across the bottom of the board and fringe them to represent grass. Pins and glue.

B. Directions for Assembly: Pin materials to the board first for placement. Staple when the arrangement is satisfactory. Cut fringe in the tops of the smaller pink petals and glue them onto the larger ones. Staple the grass across the bottom of the board. Arrange the flowers. Glue the leaves to the stems when flower placement is satisfactory. Staple flowers and title letters to the board.

4. SHADES OF SUMMER (Grades 2-8)

A. Preparation and Materials: Staple a background of your choice to the board. Cut title letters from magazine or multi-colored paper in free from style. Collect pictures of summer activities, an old window shade, assorted felt pens and glue.

B. Directions for Assembly: Staple the summer pictures to the background. Glue the title words onto the window shade and draw in the lower corner a flower with the felt pens. Attach the shade to the top of the board. If possible, make it retractable.

C. Variations: 1. Cut small shades and attach over each separate picture. Staple the title at the top of the board.

2. Attach the shade as indicated in Directions for Assembly except cut out around each picture so that the shade acts as matting.

5. SAFETY SIGNS FOR "CYCLISTS" (Grades 3-8)

A. Preparation and Materials: Staple a black background onto the board. Cut yellow block style letters to spell the title. Obtain a picture of a bicycle. Cut the traffic sign shapes from colored paper and print what each sign represents on it with felt pen.

SAFETY SIGNS
for 'CYCLISTS

WARNING
Diamond
Shaped

YIELD
Triangular
Shaped

STOP
Octagonal
Shaped

Railroad
Crossing
R R
Circular
Shaped

Rectangular or
Square Shaped
Regulatory Sign
NO
BICYCLES

1. STOP: Cut this sign from red paper in the shape of an octagon. Print on it STOP and Octagon Shaped.

2. WARNING: Cut this diamond shaped sign from yellow paper. Print on it WARNING and Diamond Shaped. Draw a right angle arrow on it.

3. YIELD: Cut this triangular shaped sign from white paper. Cut three red strips to form the border around the edges. Print on it YIELD and Triangular Shaped.

4. RAILROAD CROSSING: Cut a yellow circle and two black strips to crisscross through the center of the circle. Print two R's, Circular Shaped and Railroad Crossing on this sign.

5. REGULATORY: Cut a square and a rectangle (see illustrations) from white paper. In the center of the square draw a bicycle. Then with red felt pen draw a circle with a diagonal

line through it over the bike. Print REGULATORY RULES and Square Shaped on the square and NO BICYCLES and Rectangle Shaped on the rectangle.

B. Directions for Assembly: Staple the title and bike picture to the top of the board. Staple the traffic signs in the remaining board space.

6. FAR AWAY (Grades 5-8)

A. Preparation and Materials: Staple a black fabric or paper background to the board. Cut white block style letters from white paper. Print the following quotation on a piece of heavy white paper—

"Far away there in the sunshine
are my highest aspirations.
I may not reach them, but
I can look up and see their
beauty, believe in them,
and try to follow where
they may lead."
—Louise May Alcott

Cut a color picture of a sunset over water from a magazine or travel brochure. Gold braid and glue.

B. Directions for Assembly: Staple the quotation paper in the lower right corner and the sunset picture in the upper left corner. Glue gold braid around the picture as a frame and

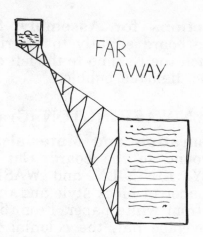

FAR
AWAY

then bring it down to the quotation as shown in the illustration. Staple the title letters in the upper right portion of the board.

7. PLAY IT COOL (Grades 6-8)

A. Preparation and Materials: Staple a blue background to the top half of the board for sky and a white background to the bottom half. Glue cotton to the white background to repre-

sent snow. Cut the igloo from white paper and add detail lines with felt pen. Cut the Eskimo from colored paper. Add features and details with felt pen. Glue on cotton dipped in brown paint or shoe polish for fur accents on the hood, suit and boots. Cut a free form cloud for the dialogue bubble and print on it PLAY IT COOL! STAY IN SCHOOL! Print the word SCHOOL over the entrance to the igloo.

B. Directions for Assembly: Staple the igloo to the board slightly to the right of the center. Attach the Eskimo to the left of the igloo and add the dialogue bubble.

8. LINCOLN-WASHINGTON (Grades 1-8)

A. Preparation and Materials: Staple a red background to the board. Cut the words FEBRUARY, LINCOLN and WASHINGTON from blue paper in block style and the numbers 12 and 22 from white paper. From black paper cut the stovepipe hat, the colonial hat and a strip to divide the board in half. Black yarn and glue.

B. Directions for Assembly: Staple the word February across the top of the board and the dividing strip through the middle beneath the letters. In the left half of the board staple the number 12, the stovepipe hat over the number and the name Lincoln at the bottom. Glue on black yarn to resemble a beard below the hat. In the right half staple the number 22, the colonial hat over the number and the name Washington at the bottom.

9. HALLOWEEN (Grades K-8)

A. Preparation and Materials: Staple a black background to the board. Cut a large orange circle for a moon. Draw a silhouette of a witch on a broom on black paper and very carefully cut it out. Glue.

B. Directions for Assembly: Staple the orange circle in the center of the black background. Glue the silhouette to the center of the circle.

C. Variation: Cut a circle from the center of a large piece of black paper. Glue a piece of orange tissue paper to the backside of the black paper. Glue the witch to the front side in the center of the orange. Attach to a window instead of the bulletin board.

10. THANKSGIVING (Grades 2-8)

A. Preparation and Materials: Staple an orange background to the board. Cut dark

brown block style letters to spell the title. Either cut feathers from many colors of paper or collect real feathers. Attach to a headband for an Indian head-dress. Cut the pilgrim hat from black paper and add a gold paper buckle. Cut two hands and glue together to resemble shaking hands. Collect many fall colored leaves and wax them, or use corn husks.

B. Directions for Assembly: Staple the leaves or husks to the board as a frame. Inside this border staple the headdress and pilgrim hat. Beneath these staple the title letters and then the hands under the title.

11. JOY TO THE WORLD (Grades K-8)

A. Preparation and Materials: Staple a black background to the board. Cut white block

style letters to spell the title. Take six ten inch diameter white paper doilies. Fold three of them in half and fold down the top third of the other three. Take the doilies that are folded down a third and lap the two edges over each other forming a cone shaped body, staple. Then staple a doily folded in half to each body for the arms. Cut three heads, draw on facial features with felt pen and add yarn hair. Tie three red bows from narrow ribbon or gift tie. Cut three red songbook shapes and fold them in half. Glue.

B. Directions for Assembly: Staple the title letters at the top and down the right side of the board. Staple the three bodies to the board, then glue on the heads and red bows. Staple the songbooks to the "Hands." This will bring the arm doilies to the front of the bodies.

12. HAPPY EASTER (Grades K-8)

A. Preparation and Materials: Staple a pastel colored background to the board. Cut title letters from a color compatible with your background in a style of your choice. Cut the bunny head with ears, paws and the egg from tagboard. Cover the bunny parts with cotton. Cut two eyes and add details with felt pen. Cut pink linings for the ears. Cover the egg with foil or gift wrap. Decorate it with scraps of rick-rack, lace, etc. Glue.

HAPPY EASTER

B. Directions for Assembly: Attach the bunny head to the board and add the egg over it. Glue on the paws. Staple or glue the title letters in the lower right corner.

C. Variation: Have scraps of material and trims in a box. Let children take turns decorating the egg.

13. RELIGIOUS CELEBRATIONS (Grades 6-8)

A. Preparation and Materials: Staple a black background to the board. Cut title letters and names of religions from gold foil in block style. Using the illustrations for patterns, cut the religious symbols also from gold foil. Print the celebration days on a piece of gold colored paper with felt pen. Glue.

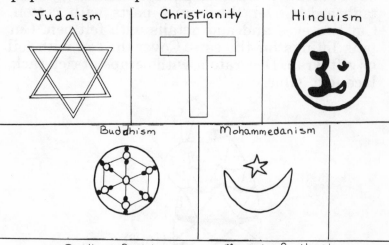

Buddha's Birthday	Mourning for Husain
Christmas	Passover
Fatima's Birthday	Ramadan
Hanukkah	Rosh Hashanah
Mohammed's Birthday	Yom Kippur

B. Directions for Assembly: Staple the title letters across the top of the board. Glue the symbols and names to the board. Staple the paper with the names of celebrations to the bottom of the board.

14. COLOR BOARD (Grades K-2)

A. Preparation and Materials: Divide the board into six equal sections vertically and staple one of the following colors to each of the sections for a background: red, orange, yellow, green, blue and violet. Cut a wide strip of white

Red	Orange	Yellow	Green	Blue	Violet

paper to fit across the top of the board. Cut block style letters to spell the colors. Cut strips of black paper to mark the divisions on the board. Collect pictures of objects that are the same colors as the section backgrounds.

B. Directions for Assembly: Staple the color letters to the white strip above the section of the same color. Staple the pictures in the appropriate section, matting them if necessary to make them show up.

C. Variation: Make the colored background sections of fiberboard or plywood so they are free standing. Attach cup hooks to these sections from which the objects can hang. Make the objects of heavy cardboard or thin wood and punch a hole in the top so they can hang from the hooks. Let the children match the objects with the color boards.

15. MONTHS (Grades K-6)

A. Preparation and Materials: Staple a white background to the board. Divide the board into twelve equal sections, one for each month. Cut black paper strips or use plastic tape to cover the dividing lines. Cut all month letters in block style.

January: Cut black letters to spell the month and a white snowflake shape. Mount the snowflake on colored paper to make it show up against the background.

February: Cut the heart and month letters from red paper.

March: Cut month letters from gold paper and the lion and lamb pictures from a magazine.

April: Cut month letters from gray paper. Then cut out a gray cloud, a black cloud and a white lightning streak. Take a piece of clear plastic wrap and shred it part way up to resemble rain. Assemble in the following order: black cloud, rain, gray cloud and lightning streak.

May: Cut month letters and flower petals from pink paper, the flower center from yellow, stem and leaves from green and a flower pot from any compatible color. Glue the petals and stem to the yellow center. Glue the leaves to the stem and the whole flower to the flowerpot.

June: Cut dark blue month letters and add an American flag, real, cut out or drawn.

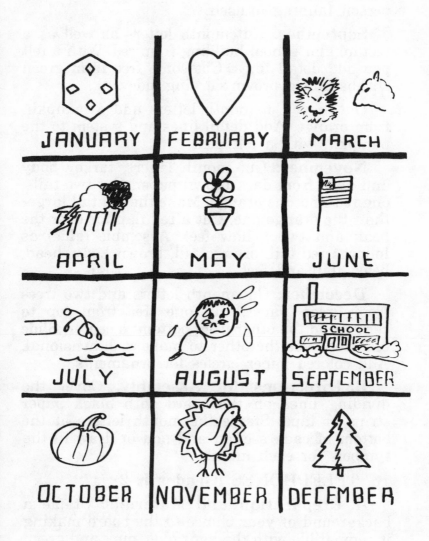

July: Cut blue month letters and use colored felt pens to draw the picture of a diving board and someone diving into the water.

August: Cut black month letters and with colored felt pens draw a cartoon of a sweltering person fanning himself.

September: Cut month letters as well as a rectangular school building from red. With a felt pen add detail lines. Cut some free form green shrubs and a brown curving sidewalk.

October: Cut month letters and a pumpkin from orange. Add detail lines and a stem to the pumpkin with a felt pen.

November: Cut month letters, turkey body and head from dark brown paper. Cut two tails, one red and one orange. Make the red tail larger than the orange one. Cut a red flap for over the beak and two yellow feet. Assemble (glue) as follows: red tail, orange tail, brown body, head, beak, flap and feet.

December: Cut month letters and two trees from green paper. Slit one tree from top to center and the other from bottom to center. Slide one tree over the other to make it dimensional. Add colored paper circles for ornaments.

B. Directions for Assembly: Cover the dividing lines on the board with black paper strips or tape. Staple the month letters at the bottom of each section and add or draw in the symbols for each month.

16. TELEPHONES (Grades K-2)

A. Preparation and Materials: Staple a background of your choice to the board making it compatible with the light blue, pink and green

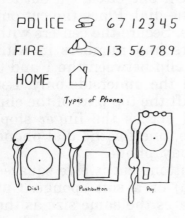

POLICE ☎ 67 12345

FIRE ⬦ 13 56789

HOME ⌂

Types of Phones

Dial   Pushbutton   Pay

suggested for the three phones. Cut three strips of white paper to fit across the width of the board. On one strip with felt pen print the word POLICE, draw a policeman's hat (or a policeman), and write the telephone number of your local police station. On another with felt pen print the word FIRE, draw a fireman's hat and write the number of your local fire department. On the third with felt pen print the word HOME, draw a house, but leave the telephone number blank. Cut black block style letters to spell TYPES OF PHONES, DIAL, PUSHBUTTON and PAY.

To make the dial phone, cut the base and receiver from light blue paper. Glue a piece of Velcro to the center of the back side of the receiver and the top of the base. Punch a hole in the left side of the receiver and base top. Add a piece of yarn or gift tie for the cord. Make the push-button phone exactly the same way as you made the dial phone but in pink. To make the pay phone cut the receiver and rectangular base from light green paper. Glue on the Velcro and attach the cord. Cut three small graduated circles for coin slots and a small rectangle for the coin return from aluminum foil. Glue these to the base.

To make the circular dials, cut two identical circles of white paper. On one circle cut out ten small finger holes for the dial. Place the cut out dial over the solid circle. Secure the centers with a brad. Print the letters and numbers in with felt pen. Place a paper clip between the 1 and 0 and glue it in place on the underside only. Let the glue set. Carefully lift the top part of the clip away from the dial to act as the finger stop. Make two of these dials, one for the dial phone and the other for the pay phone.

To make the push-buttons cut twelve squares of thin foam (art foam) or a soft sponge. Cut twelve white paper squares the same size as the foam squares and print the letters and numbers on them. Glue the paper squares onto the foam squares, then onto the rectangular push-button base and then onto the base of the phone.

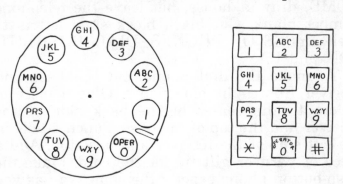

B. Directions for Assembly: Staple the three strips of paper to the top of the board in this order: POLICE first, FIRE second and HOME third. Beneath these strips staple the words TYPES OF PHONES. Staple the phones and their names to the board. Add the dials to the dial and pay phones. Be sure that you have left the receivers operable.

17. TELEPHONE DIRECTORIES
(Grades 3-8)

A. Preparation and Materials: Staple a black background to the board. Cut a piece of white paper to fit the board diagonally corner to corner, left to right. Print the words TELEPHONE DIRECTORIES in black on this white paper. (Caution:

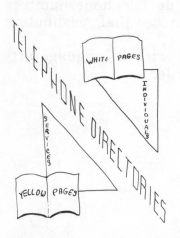

Do this very lightly in pencil first. All lines, except for vertical lines, should be on the same diagonal as paper.) Cut a square of white paper in two diagonally corner to corner. Print the word INDIVIDUALS vertically in black on the right section of the square. On the left section print the word SERVICES vertically in black.

Using an old phone book tear out a small section from both the white and yellow pages. Write the words WHITE, PAGES, YELLOW and PAGES on pieces of white paper, one word on each piece.

B. Directions for Assembly: Staple the diagonal white paper with TELEPHONE DIRECTORIES on it to the board. In the upper right hand segment attach the triangle with INDIVIDUALS on it to the board. Then pin the white pages to the board. Draw the corners in a bit to the center to give a more natural open-book effect. Attach the paper with WHITE on it to the left half of the open pages and the paper with PAGES to the right half. In the lower left segment attach the triangle with SERVICES on it. Then add the yellow pages and complete in the same manner as for the white pages.

C. Suggestions for Use: 1. Combine bulletin boards 16 and 17 from this section into a lesson on how to look up telephone numbers and services, and how to use dial, pushbutton and pay phones.

2. This could be used with a language arts lesson on alphabetical order.

PUT-ONS

1. Use scraps of colored paper, fabric, etc., to make a patchwork effect for a background. Use this as an announcement board.

2. Have children or teacher make or purchase holiday decorations, such as; shamrocks, turkeys, etc.

3. "This is your week board" — Pick children's names from a hat. Child whose name is selected may fix the bulletin board as he chooses. (To avoid wasted time, pick names one week in advance and keep a check on the child's progress.)

4. September welcome board — Draw smile faces. Under each write the name of each child to be in the class.

5. September — Scramble letters of extracurricular activities, teachers names, children's names, etc.

6. Hobby Board — Feature a different hobby each week. Have children contribute their ideas, projects, etc. Use as an interest stimulator.

7. Put up copies of international street signs. (Get from the secretary of state office.)

8. Put up posters of bicycle and kite safety. (Get from state safety department or county extension service.)

9. Put up fun pictures of student activities. Take pictures of children at recess, on field trips or any candid shots. Have children supply pictures or cut magazine pictures.

10. Make a chess board and have velcro in each square. Put velcro on chess pieces also.

11. Put up pictures of cars, trucks, scenery, seasons, etc.

12. Put up vacation activity pictures.

13. Put up greeting cards.

14. Put up any background. Gather together many old selfstick bows and arrange in various shapes (animals, circles, faces, etc.).

15. Copy slogans, sayings, etc., onto pieces of paper and attach to the board or write directly on the board.

Examples:

"Don't be afraid to ask dumb questions. They're easier to handle than dumb mistakes."
—Unknown—

"A man's life consists not of what he has, but what he is."
—Unknown—

"Don't be conceited: even postage stamps become useless when they get stuck on themselves."
—Unknown—

"Make someone happy — mind your own business."
—Unknown—

"If all the year were playing holidays, to sport would be as tedious as to work."
—Shakespeare—

"The greatest thing in this world is not so much where we started as in what direction we are moving."
—Oliver W. Holmes—

SECTION VII: "LETTERING"

This section will show you how to make the different styles of lettering.

LETTERING

Lettering need not be fancy to be effective. In the primary grades or for children with learning disabilities, the lettering should be simple and clear to aid in letter recognition.

1. CONSTRUCTION

A. Block Letters: Basic Cuts 1

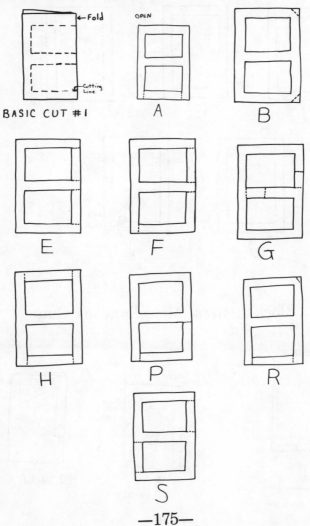

BASIC CUT #1 A B

E F G

H P R

S

Block Letters: Basic Cuts 2

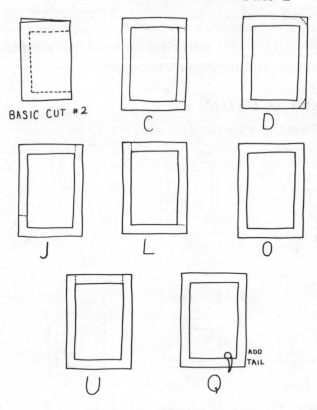

BASIC CUT #2

C

D

J

L

O

U

Q

ADD TAIL

Block Letters: Miscellaneous Cuts

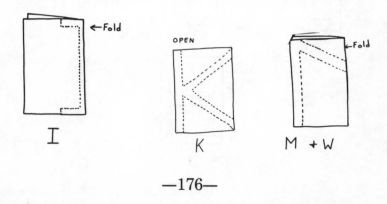

←Fold

I

OPEN

K

←Fold

M + W

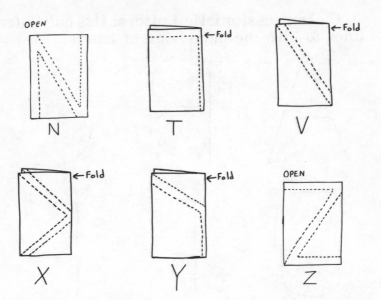

B. Free Form Letters: Following no special pattern, cut letters in recognizable shapes.

C. Impressionistic Letters: Use only a few lines to give the impression of letters.

M N C

P Q R

S T U

V W X

Y Z

D. Print Letters: Cut letters from magazines or cut letters from newspaper headlines. Use a variety of sizes and colors. (Classroom helpers could be given the task of cutting out these letters.) Keep the individual letters in separate boxes or envelopes for future use.

MaTh

E. Shadow-box Letters: Cut two identical sets of letters. After attaching the first set to the board, there are two ways to complete the shadow-box. Stick a pin through the second set and pin to the first set leaving a space between them or accordion-pleat strips of paper and glue ends to the letter sets. Use a stiff paper for the accordion-pleats, don't make them too long or the outer letters will droop.

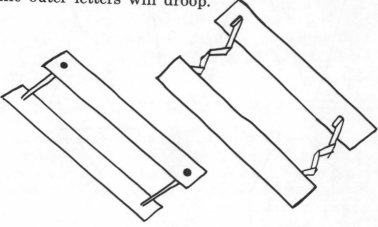

F. Torn Letters: Using any of the lettering styles mentioned, tear the letters instead of cutting them out with scissors.

2. MATERIALS

A. Tagboard or Heavy Paper: Cut block letters from tagboard or other heavy paper. To do this, make sample letters using the patterns in Block Letters. Trace letters onto the heavy paper and cut with sharp scissors or a knife.

B. Writing Utensils: Write or print directly on the background with felt pen, crayon or chalk using any lettering style. If chalk is used, spray with fixative to prevent smearing.

C. Yarn or String: Staple, pin or glue yarn or string to the board in block print or cursive letters. To make letters more durable, dip these materials in heavy starch or glue, form letters and let dry on a flat surface. Be careful where you put the letters to dry if glue is used so they can be removed when dry.

D. Masking or Plastic Tape: Form letters using a style from the previous lettering patterns with either tape material. The plastic tape will give you color variety.

E. Foam Cartons or Trays: Cut letters using a style from the previous lettering patterns out of the plastic foam egg cartons or meat trays.

F. Toothpicks or Popsicle Sticks: Form letters with toothpicks or popsicle sticks. Glue directly to the board, glue sticks together and then attach to the board or glue sticks to heavy paper in title form.

3. GUIDE LINES

Anytime you are printing or writing, use guidelines before making the letters. In other words, draw three faint lines an equal distance apart. Form letters between these lines. Carefully erase lines when letters are made.

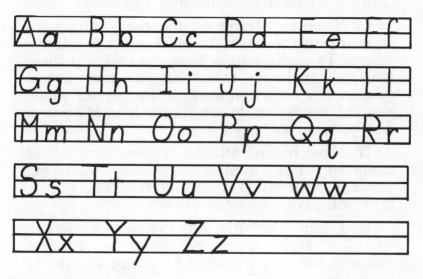

4. PLACEMENT

To determine letter placement, count the number of letters and spaces in the title. Decide on the middle letter or space. If it is a letter, attach that letter and work from that center to the ends.

Example: THE EARTH

There are eight letters and a space. The middle letter is "E" from the word "EARTH." Attach it and then put up the remaining letters. Be sure to leave a space to separate the words.

If the center is a space, attach the two letters that surround the space and continue in the same manner.

Example: THE SEA

There are six letters and a space. The space is the center. Attach both the "E" from the word "THE" and the "S" from the word "SEA" on either side of the middle space.

This letter placement method will work either vertically or horizontally.

INDEX

TITLE	K	1	2	3	4	5	6	7	8	PAGE
SECTION I: "BULLETIN BOARD READINESS"										
General Information										3
Special Boards										6
Materials										7
SECTION II: "LANGUAGE ARTS"										
1. Vowels	x	x	x	x						13
2. Feel The Word	x	x	x							13
3. Sight Words	x	x	x							14
4. Odd Man Out		x	x	x	x	x				15
5. Make Your Word Garden Grow				x	x	x	x	x	x	16
6. Where Shall I Look?					x	x	x	x	x	17
7. Critical Thinking					x	x	x	x	x	19
8. SQ3R = Better Learning							x	x	x	20
9. Newspaper Services							x	x	x	21
10. Want Ads							x	x	x	22
11. Potpourri	x	x	x	x	x	x	x	x	x	23
12. Jiminy Cricket!		x	x	x	x	x	x	x	x	24
13. Good Spelling				x	x	x	x	x	x	25
14. Foolish And Funny			x	x	x	x	x	x	x	25
15. Comic Caper				x	x	x	x	x	x	26
16. Superstitions				x	x	x	x	x	x	27
17. How Wise R U?					x	x	x	x	x	28
18. Brew Up An Interest In Reading				x	x	x	x	x	x	29
19. A Good Listener				x	x	x	x	x	x	31
20. How Do We Listen?				x	x	x	x	x	x	31
21. Spelling Scramble				x	x	x	x	x	x	33
22. Monster Of The Day!				x	x	x	x	x	x	33
23. Don't Be Spooked!				x	x	x	x	x	x	34
24. Prefixes				x	x	x	x	x	x	35
25. Compound Words			x	x	x	x	x	x	x	36
26. Antonyms Are An Open And Shut Case				x	x	x	x	x	x	37
27. Homonyms				x	x	x	x	x	x	38
28. Dictionary Daisies					x	x	x	x	x	39
29. Mail Call		x	x							41
30. Punctuation			x	x	x	x	x	x	x	42
31. Good Grammar				x	x	x	x	x	x	44
32. Make A Sentence				x	x	x	x	x	x	45
33. Paragraph Wagon				x	x	x	x	x	x	46
34. Parts Of Speech Names						x	x	x	x	46
35. Parts Of Speech Uses						x	x	x	x	47
36. Haiku					x	x	x	x	x	49

GRADE LEVEL

TITLE	K	1	2	3	4	5	6	7	8	PAGE
37. Books We Read					x	x	x	x	x	50
38. The Web Of Mystery				x	x	x	x	x	x	51
39. Sign In Please!				x	x	x	x	x	x	52
40. The Library Windmill Of My Mind					x	x	x	x	x	53
41. The Card Catalog					x	x	x	x	x	54

SECTION III: "SOCIAL STUDIES"

TITLE	K	1	2	3	4	5	6	7	8	PAGE
1. Community Helpers	x	x	x	x						57
2. Tools We Use	x	x	x	x						58
3. What Shall I Be?	x	x	x	x	x					58
4. Transportation	x	x	x	x						59
5. Our Place On The Earth					x	x	x	x	x	60
6. Hang In There					x	x	x	x	x	61
7. Latitude And Longitude						x	x	x	x	62
8. The United States				x	x	x	x	x	x	64
9. Indians Of North America				x	x	x	x	x	x	65
10. Secrets Of Plymouth Rock				x	x	x	x	x	x	66
11. Early Colonial Life				x	x	x	x	x	x	67
12. Portraits Of Liberty				x	x	x	x	x	x	68
13. Presidents				x	x	x	x	x	x	69
14. Revoltin' Reasons					x	x	x	x	x	69
15. The Civil War					x	x	x	x	x	70
16. World Wars					x	x	x	x	x	71
17. Wartime					x	x	x	x	x	72
18. Who Stepped Where				x	x	x	x	x	x	73
19. Our Government						x	x	x	x	74
20. Capital Cities					x	x	x	x	x	75
21. Around The World					x	x	x	x	x	77
22. Royalty						x	x	x	x	77
23. People And Places				x	x	x	x	x		78
24. Collage				x	x	x	x	x	x	79
25. Light Up A Fact				x	x	x	x	x	x	79

SECTION IV: "MATH"

TITLE	K	1	2	3	4	5	6	7	8	PAGE
1. Add The Dominoes	x	x	x	x						83
2. Counting	x	x	x	x						83
3. Number Folks		x	x	x	x	x	x	x	x	85
4. Place Value				x	x	x	x	x	x	86
5. Mayan Numbers					x	x	x	x	x	87
6. Roman Numerals		x	x	x	x	x	x	x	x	88
7. Big And Little	x	x	x							89
8. What Do You Mean?			x	x	x	x	x	x	x	90
9. Sets		x	x	x	x	x	x	x	x	90
10. Grocery Shopping		x	x	x	x	x	x	x	x	91
11. Time Tables			x	x	x	x	x			93
12. Division Talk			x	x	x	x	x	x	x	96
13. Fractions				x	x	x	x	x	x	97

—186—

	TITLE	GRADE LEVEL								PAGE
		K	1	2	3	4	5	6	7 8	
14.	The Puzzle Of Fractions			x	x	x	x	x	x	98
15.	Equivalents					x	x	x	x	99
16.	Ratio			x	x	x	x	x	x	100
17.	Money	x	x	x	x					101
18.	Banking					x	x	x	x	102
19.	Calendar Time			x	x	x	x	x	x	103
20.	Telling Time			x	x	x	x	x	x	104
21.	Measurement			x	x	x	x	x	x	105
22.	The Metric System			x	x	x	x	x	x	106
23.	Geometric Figures			x	x	x	x	x	x	107
24.	P = Perimeter					x	x	x	x	108
25.	A = Area					x	x	x	x	109
26.	Area Of A Circle					x	x	x	x	110
27.	Bone Up On _____			x	x	x	x	x	x	111
28.	Snow Job				x	x	x	x	x	113

SECTION V: "SCIENCE"

1.	The Animal Kingdom			x	x	x	x	x	x	117
2.	Be Informed About Biological Sciences				x	x	x	x	x	117
3.	Undersea World			x	x	x	x	x	x	118
4.	Classification Of Plants					x	x	x	x	119
5.	Tree Talk					x	x	x	x	121
6.	Flower Parts					x	x	x	x	122
7.	Open The Doors To Good Nutrition			x	x	x	x			123
8.	Good Health			x	x	x	x	x	x	125
9.	Good Grooming			x	x	x	x	x	x	126
10.	Brush Your Teeth Often		x	x	x	x	x	x	x	127
11.	Cross Section Of A Tooth				x	x	x	x	x	128
12.	Blood				x	x	x	x	x	129
13.	Add-A-Bone						x	x	x	130
14.	Fluoroscope				x	x	x	x	x	131
15.	Puzzle Of The Mind						x	x	x	132
16.	The Physical Sciences				x	x	x	x	x	132
17.	Chemical Elements					x	x	x	x	133
18.	Heat				x	x	x	x	x	134
19.	Thermometers				x	x	x	x	x	135
20.	Magnets			x	x	x	x	x	x	136
21.	Rocks					x	x	x	x	137
22.	Treasures Of The Earth				x	x	x	x	x	138
23.	Weather Map				x	x	x	x	x	138
24.	Precipitation					x	x	x	x	139
25.	Speed Of Light						x	x	x	140
26.	Beyond The Earth					x	x	x	x	141
27.	The Universe			x	x	x	x	x	x	142
28.	Look Up			x	x	x	x	x	x	143
29.	A Prism					x	x	x	x	144
30.	Ecology				x	x	x	x	x	145

	TITLE		GRADE LEVEL									PAGE
		K	1	2	3	4	5	6	7	8	
31.	Ecology Is Now					x	x	x	x	x	146
32.	Bright Ideas					x	x	x	x	x	147

SECTION VI: "JUST BECAUSE"

	TITLE	K	1	2	3	4	5	6	7	8	PAGE
1.	Fall	x	x	x	x	x	x	x	x	x	151
2.	Wintertime Is Funtime	x	x	x	x	x	x	x	x	x	151
3.	Spring Is Here!	x	x	x	x	x	x	x	x	x	152
4.	Shades Of Summer			x	x	x	x	x	x	x	153
5.	Safety Signs For "Cyclists"				x	x	x	x	x	x	154
6.	Far Away						x	x	x	x	156
7.	Play It Cool							x	x	x	157
8.	Lincoln-Washington		x	x	x	x	x	x	x	x	158
9.	Halloween	x	x	x	x	x	x	x	x	x	159
10.	Thanksgiving			x	x	x	x	x	x	x	159
11.	Joy To The World	x	x	x	x	x	x	x	x	x	160
12.	Happy Easter	x	x	x	x	x	x	x	x	x	161
13.	Religious Celebrations							x	x	x	162
14.	Color Board	x	x	x							163
15.	Months	x	x	x	x	x	x	x			164
16.	Telephones	x	x	x							166
17.	Telephone Directories				x	x	x	x	x	x	169
18.	Put-Ons										171

SECTION VII: "LETTERING"

		PAGE
	Lettering	175

Back to basics & the Spice Series

MATHEMATICS

- ☐ **PLUS** — Primary Mathematics ● Grades K-4
- ☐ **Plus Volume I** ● Grades K-2 Duplicators from **PLUS**
- ☐ **Plus Volume II** ● Grades 2-4 Duplicators from **PLUS**
- ☐ **CHALLENGE** — Intermediate Mathematics ● Grades 4-8
- ☐ **Challenge Volume I** ● Grades 4-6 Duplicators from **CHALLENGE**
- ☐ **Challenge Volume II** ● Grades 6-8 Duplicators from **CHALLENGE**

METRIC SYSTEM

- ☐ **METER** — Converting to the Metric System ● Grades K-8
- ☐ **Meter Volume I** ● Grades K-3 Duplicators Introducing Metrics
- ☐ **Meter Volume II** ● Grades 3-6 Duplicators from **METER**
- ☐ **Meter Volume III** ● Grades 6-8 Duplicators from **METER**

SOCIAL STUDIES

- ☐ **SPARK** — **Primary Social Studies** ● Grades K-4
- ☐ **Spark Volume I** ● Grades K-2 Duplicators from **SPARK**
- ☐ **Spark Volume II** ● Grades 2-4 Duplicators from **SPARK**
- ☐ **FOCUS** — **Intermediate Social Studies** ● Grades 4-8
- ☐ **Focus Volume I** ● Grades 4-6 Duplicators from **FOCUS**
- ☐ **Focus Volume II** ● Grades 6-8 Duplicators from **FOCUS**
- ☐ **CHOICE** — **Elementary Economics** ● Grades K-8
- ☐ **CAREER** — **Elementary Career Education** ● Grades K-8
- ☐ **PRIDE** — **Elementary Black Studies** ● Grades K-8

SPECIALTY STUDIES

- ☐ **CREATE** — Primary Art ● Grades K-4
- ☐ **CRAFT** — Intermediate Art ● Grades 4-8
- ☐ **NOTE** — Elementary Music ● Grades K-8
- ☐ **GROWTH** — Elementary Health ● Grades K-8
- ☐ **PREVENT** — Elementary Safety ● Grades K-8
- ☐ **Prevent Volume I** ● Grades K-4 Duplicators from **PREVENT**
- ☐ **Prevent Volume II** ● Grades 4-8 Duplicators from **PREVENT**
- ☐ **STAGE** — Elementary Dramatics ● Grades K-8
- ☐ **ACTION** — Elementary Physical Education ● Grades K-8
- ☐ **DISPLAY** — Elementary Bulletin Board Ideas ● Grades K-8

PRESCHOOL AND KINDERGARTEN READINESS

- ☐ **LAUNCH** — Reading & Math Readiness ● Colors ● Muscle Builders
- ☐ **Launch Volume I** ● Duplicators from **LAUNCH**
- ☐ **Launch Volume II** ● Additional Duplicators from **LAUNCH**

MORE TITLES AVAILABLE ● SEE FOLLOWING PAGE

See your local School Supply Dealer
or mail to

The SPICE® Series
EDUCATIONAL SERVICE, INC.

What is "The Spice Series"?

The "series", with each book having it's own title, was founded upon the theory that all teachers can use simple and explicit ideas to enrich any program. These ideas are produced in book form at a cost of $5.25 each. From the idea books, came the pre-printed duplicators ready for student use. The duplicator books are 40 pages and also $5.25 each.

LANGUAGE ARTS

☐ **SPICE** — Primary Language Arts ● Grades K-4
☐ **Spice Volume I** ● Grades K-2 Duplicators from **SPICE**
☐ **Spice Volume II** ● Grades 2-4 Duplicators from **SPICE**
☐ **ANCHOR** — Intermediate Language Arts ● Grades 4-8
☐ **Anchor Volume I** ● Grades 4-6 Duplicators from **ANCHOR**
☐ **Anchor Volume II** ● Grades 6-8 Duplicators from **ANCHOR**
☐ **RESCUE** — Elementary Remedial Reading
☐ **Rescue Volume I** ● Grades K-8 Duplicators from **RESCUE**
☐ **FLAIR** — Elementary Creative Writing
☐ **Flair Volume I** ● Grades K-8 Duplicators from **FLAIR**
☐ **SCRIBE** — Elementary Handwriting

ORGANIZE A LIBRARY & DICTIONARY STUDY PROGRAM BY USING THE FOLLOWING DUPLICATORS

LIBRARY STUDY — LINGO & LOCATION ● CARDS & CATALOGS ● RESEARCH
☐ **Library Studies Volume I** ● Grades 3-6
☐ **Library Studies Volume II** ● Grades 7-9

DICTIONARY STUDY — WORD USE & ORDER ● SYLLABLES & SPELLING
☐ **Dictionary Studies Volume I** ● Single letters Grades K-2
☐ **Dictionary Studies Volume II** ● Letter combinations Grades K-2
☐ **Dictionary Studies Volume III** ● Grades 3-6
☐ **Dictionary Studies Volume IV** ● Grades 7-9

SCIENCE

☐ **PROBE** — Primary Science ● Grades K-4
☐ **Probe Volume I** ● Grades K-2 Duplicators from **PROBE**
☐ **Probe Volume II** ● Grades 2-4 Duplicators from **PROBE**
☐ **INQUIRE** — Intermediate Science ● Grades 4-8
☐ **Inquire Volume I** ● Duplicators from **INQUIRE**
☐ **ECO** — Elementary Ecology ● Grades K-8

MORE TITLES AVAILABLE ● PRECEDING PAGE

Pricing subject to change without notice. Individual orders must be accompanied by payment. Foreign orders must be accompanied by full payment including a 10% handling charge. We pay all shipping costs, Regular Mail, Domestic Mail only.

School Name _____

School Address _____

City _____ State _____ Zip _____

Person Ordering _____

If you wish to have your order shipped to your home, please attach your home address on a separate card.